BIBLIOASIS INTERNATIONAL TRANSLATION

General Editor: Stephen Henighan

1 *I Wrote Stone: The Selected Poetry of Ryszard Kapuściński* (Poland)
  Translated by Diana Kuprel and Marek Kusiba

2 *Good Morning Comrades* by Ondjaki (Angola)
  Translated by Stephen Henighan

3 *Kahn & Engelmann* by Hans Eichner (Austria-Canada)
  Translated by Jean M. Snook

4 *Dance with Snakes* by Horacio Castellanos Moya (El Salvador)
  Translated by Lee Paula Springer

5 *Black Alley* by Mauricio Segura (Quebec)
  Translated by Dawn M. Cornelio

6 *The Accident* by Mihail Sebastian (Romania)
  Translated by Stephen Henighan

7 *Love Poems* by Jaime Sabines (Mexico)
  Translated by Colin Carberry

8 *The End of the Story* by Liliana Heker (Argentina)
  Translated by Andrea G. Labinger

9 *The Tuner of Silences* by Mia Couto (Mozambique)
  Translated by David Brookshaw

10 *For as Far as the Eye Can See* by Robert Melançon (Quebec)
  Translated by Judith Cowan

11 *Eucalyptus* by Mauricio Segura (Quebec)
  Translated by Donald Winkler

12 *Granma Nineteen and the Soviet's Secret* by Ondjaki (Angola)
  Translated by Stephen Henighan

13 *Montreal Before Spring* by Robert Melançon (Quebec)
  Translated by Donald McGrath

14 *Pensativities: Essays and Provocations* by Mia Couto (Mozambique)
  Translated by David Brookshaw

15 *Arvida* by Samuel Archibald (Quebec)
  Translated by Donald Winkler

AGAINST AMAZON

Against Amazon

AND OTHER ESSAYS

Jorge Carrión

TRANSLATED FROM THE SPANISH
BY PETER BUSH

BIBLIOASIS
Windsor, Ontario

First published as *Contra Amazon* by Galaxia Gutenberg, Barcelona, Spain 2019.
Copyright © Jorge Carrión, 2019

Translation copyright © Peter Bush, 2020

FIRST EDITION

ISBN 978-1-77196-303-9 (Trade Paper)
ISBN 978-1-77196-304-6 (eBook)

Title: Against Amazon : and other essays / Jorge Carrión ; translated from the Spanish by Peter Bush.
Other titles: Contra Amazon. English
Names: Carrión, Jorge, 1976- author.
Series: Biblioasis international translation series; no. 32.
Description: Series statement: Biblioasis international translation series ; no. 32 | Translation of: Contra Amazon.
Identifiers: Canadiana (ebook) 20200154095 | Canadiana (print) 20200154060 | ISBN 9781771963046 (ebook) | ISBN 9781771963039 (softcover)
Subjects: LCSH: Amazon.com (Firm) | LCSH: Internet bookstores. | LCSH: Bookstores. | LCSH: Bookstores—Social aspects. | LCSH: Electronic commerce. | LCSH: Electronic commerce—Social aspects. | LCSH: Booksellers and bookselling.
Classification: LCC Z278.1568 C3713 2020 | DDC 381/.4500202854678—dc23

Edited by Stephen Henighan and Daniel Wells
Copyedited by Emily Donaldson
Text designed and set in Borges Blanca by Tetragon, London

This book has been published with a subsidy from the Ministry of Culture and Sport of Spain.
Printed in Canada

Contents

Author's Note

Contra Amazon. Siete razones / un manifiesto ("Against Amazon. Seven reasons / a manifesto") was published online by *Jot Down Magazine* in April 2017. The Spanish magazine also printed several hundred posters that were sent to bookshops throughout Spain. They can still be found, framed, in Rata Corner in Palma de Mallorca, and in the corners of other front line bookshops. In November that same year it appeared in English, translated by Peter Bush, digitally on *Literary Hub* and on paper in a beautiful hand-sewn pamphlet the Canadian publishing house Biblioasis sent to three hundred bookshops and journalists during the launch of *Bookshops* in America and Canada. The chapbook aroused such interest that my publisher, Dan Wells, ended up giving away almost five thousand copies to professionals in the trade across the world. It was also published in Portuguese in a translation by the Brazilian writer Reginaldo Pujol in the newspaper *Folha de São Paulo*. When *Publishers Weekly* focused on the unexpectedly international phenomenon in May 2018, Dan and I spoke on the phone and decided to put together this book, which immediately won the support of Joan Tarrida, my Spanish publisher. I began at once to assemble and read all the articles, essays, interviews, and chronicles I had published on the world of books in recent years. I selected the best ones. To my surprise, the word "Amazon" appeared in many of them. Alberto Manguel had even told me at one point, without my having asked him the question, "I don't buy from Amazon," as if this were a necessary stance. Which camp are you in?

It seems impossible to write about activity in the world of books in the twenty-first century, about independent bookshops and the most innovative, challenging libraries, or the constellations of readers who remain faithful to the printed book, without thinking of Amazon as our adversary. Although Google Books and other big platforms have also influenced the ways in which we relate to texts, the multinational logistics firm headed by Jeff Bezos has become the most iconic and strident brand, the one that has violently changed—and often damaged—the traditional relationships between reader and book. Amazon is a tentacled monster that continually grows and innovates. If a few details in my manifesto have become obsolete, its spirit remains relevant. At the beginning of 2019, thanks to the struggle led by Democratic Congresswoman Alexandria Ocasio-Cortez, New York City rejected the plan to give Amazon $3.4 billion in incentives to set up a base there. Since then, when you key "against Amazon" into a search engine, it's no longer just my manifesto that appears. In a parallel development, there has been a proliferation of Amazon deliverers roaming our streets with their big backpacks, as well as those working for other companies that, in their own ways, are equally disruptive. In neo-liberal style, they have made the precarious habits of the poor who collect cardboard and scrap metal their own.

I wrote *Bookshops* in 2012, never imagining that it would be runner-up for the Anagrama Essay Prize or that it would be published in so many languages and read throughout the world, thanks to the initial commitment of Christopher MacLehose. I have continued to visit bookshops across five continents and study their histories. Thanks to the translations, I have been able to return to some of the world's best bookshops and add others, most of them remarkable, to my collection. I still haven't visited in person what is probably the most important bookshop in my life: Biblioasis in Windsor, Ontario, with its black awning, wonderful books selection, and team of booksellers and editors who were the first to take an interest in publishing *Bookshops* beyond the frontiers of my country, though I have often virtually walked along Wyandotte Street, looked at the program poster outside the Olde Walkerville Theatre, fantasized about eating New Orleans cuisine at Nola's, and finally come to a halt outside the bookshop entrance. The same grey car is always parked by the door in the Google Street View photographs.

In recent years I've developed a passion for visiting the oldest, most original or striking libraries in the cities to which I travel. Books circulate around a quadrangle whose vertices are publishers, bookshops, and private and public libraries. We readers are in the centrifugal centre of that non-stop traffic. You only have to visit your local library to realize that not every scrap of information is to be found on the internet. I remembered something even more crucial in Argentina's National Library, Melbourne's Victoria State Library, Seoul's Hyundai Card Libraries, Tokyo's International Library of Children's Literature, or Beijing's fantastic Kids Republic bookshop, which offers books and other things to touch: the experiences these spaces offer you do *not* have a digital equivalent. It is why the children's sections of bookshops and libraries are also incredibly impor-tant: they have the power to shape the readers and users of the future. Novels, films, comics, and television constantly imagine bookish spaces—both in realist mode and in fantasy and sci-fi narratives—because the convergence of discourse and object, virtual and physical, mind and body, is what makes us human.

Thanks to the translations of *Bookshops*—or maybe they are to blame—I have also discovered dark corners in some of the world's most famous bookshops. The touristy, beautiful Lello in Porto doesn't sell the Portuguese edition, *Livrarias*, apparently because some of the details I mention about the store—culled from their web page—are incorrect, and, above all, because my publishers refused to put an image of their bookshop on the book's cover. And Shakespeare & Company doesn't sell the French or English editions because they recount the true story of George Whitman and refer to other books, which they don't sell either, as sources. Censorship is everywhere. Amazon and the huge digital platforms aren't our only adversaries. We must continue reading and travelling. And always stay on the alert.

—JORGE CARRIÓN
Barcelona, April 2019

Against Amazon: Seven Arguments

∿ A MANIFESTO

I BECAUSE I DON'T WANT TO BE AN ACCOMPLICE TO SYMBOLIC EXPROPRIATION

For fifty-five years that building in Barcelona, one of the city's few examples of modern industrial architecture, was the head office of publishers Gustavo Gili. Now, after a refurbishment costing several million euros, it has become Amazon's local centre of operations. Thanks to the technology of efficiency and immediacy that it houses, Barcelona is now one of forty-five cities in the world where the company guarantees delivery of products in an hour. The Canuda bookshop, which closed in 2013 after over eighty years of existence, is now a gigantic Mango clothing store. The Catalònia bookshop, after over a hundred, is now a McDonald's with kitschy modernist decor. Expropriation is literal and physical, but also symbolic.

Typing "Amazon bookshop" into Google yields dozens of links to Amazon pages selling bookshelves. As I will never tire of repeating: Amazon is not a bookshop, it is a hypermarket. Its

1

warehouses store books next to toasters, toys, or skateboards. In its new physical bookshops, books are placed face up, because they only display the six thousand books most sought after by their customers, far fewer than the number on the shelves of genuine bookshops that are prepared to take risks. Amazon is now considering whether to repeat the same operation with a chain of small supermarkets; as far as it is concerned, there is no difference between a cultural institution and an establishment that sells food and other goods.

Jeff Bezos has a history of lengthy, symbolic expropriations. He opted to sell books rather than electrical goods because he saw a niche in the market: no bookshop could accommodate his plan to offer every single title available. In the 1990s, there were few large-scale competitors (mainly Barnes & Noble and Borders) and distributors that had adapted to the digital age by incorporating ISBN numbers into their catalogues, which is why Bezos took an American Booksellers Association course and, in record time, appropriated the prestige books had accumulated over centuries.

Even today, when Amazon produces television series, offers music online, stocks spare parts for cars and motorcycles, and is considering getting into the prepaid cell-phone business, people continue to associate the brand with the object and symbol we call a *book*. Kindle, from its launch in 2007, has imitated the form and tone of ink and the printed page. Fortunately, for the moment they can't reproduce the vegetable feel or smell of lignin on screen. Whether we like it or not, we still cannot remember with the same precision what we read on a screen: architectural transitions happen quickly; mental transitions, less so.

II   BECAUSE WE ARE ALL CYBORGS,
BUT NOT ROBOTS

We all carry implants.

We all depend on that prosthetic: our cell phone.

We are all cyborgs: mainly human, slightly mechanical.

But we do not want to be robots.

The work Amazon employees do is robotic. It was ever thus: in 1994, the five people working in Jeff Bezos's garage in Seattle were already obsessed with speed. The company has remained that way for twenty years, with many employees telling stories of stress, harassment, and inhuman work conditions, all to achieve a horrendous, machine-like efficiency.

The Amazonians are now helped by Kiva robots capable of lifting 340-kilo loads and that can move a metre and a half per second. Synchronized with the human labour force via an algorithm, their job is to lift shelves to facilitate product collection. After being gathered by the Kiva robots, purchased items move along a huge conveyor belt to the SLAM system (Scan, Label, Apply, Manifest), which performs the scanning and packaging.

Kiva robots and the SLAM system are the result of years of research. Amazon commissioned robot competitions at the International Conference on Robotics and Automation held in Seattle to perfect the processing of orders. Machines designed by MIT or the Technical University in Berlin competed to collect a rubber duck, a bag of Oreos, a toy dog, and a book in the shortest possible time. For Amazon, there is no substantial difference between those four items. They are equivalent commodities.

But not for us.

Amazon has gradually eliminated the human factor from its operations. In the early years, it employed people to write reviews of the books it sold; now the process of producing and placing a self-published book on their website isn't even mediated. Amazon has robotized the chain of distribution and wants us, the consumers, to do the same.

But we won't.

Because, for us, a book is a book is a book.

And reading a book—whether by choice or because it was given as a present—is a rite, the echo of an echo of an echo of something once sacred.

III BECAUSE I REJECT HYPOCRISY

It's to the great shame of Barcelona, a city with many excellent bookshops, that for twenty-four years the Europa Bookshop, run by the neo-Nazi Pedro Varela, was an important centre for the diffusion of anti-Semitic ideology. Fortunately, it closed down last September. Amazon sells a huge number of *Mein Kampf* editions, many with highly dubious prologues and notes. In fact, the World Jewish Congress has alerted the company to the dozens of negationist books it makes available with no obstacle to purchase. In other words, the Europa Bookshop was closed down for inciting hatred, amongst other crimes, but Amazon hasn't been, even though it's a crime to deny the Holocaust in many of the countries where it operates.

Amazon's defence is that it is against censorship. That's why it kept selling, despite the hue and cry, *The Pedophile's Guide to Love and Pleasure: A Child-lover's Code of Conduct*, by Phillip R. Greaves, although the title was eventually withdrawn. Something similar happened with *Understanding Loved Boys and Boylovers* by David L. Riegel. Amazon used the same anti-censorship argument to defend books promoting the sensual love of children as it did for books promoting Nazi ideas. But the truth is that it censors or privileges books to suit its own interests. During its dispute with the Hachette Book Group in 2014, Hachette writer Ursula K. Le Guin denounced the fact that during the conflict her books were more difficult to find on Amazon.

Apparently the only thing that matters to Amazon is the speed and efficiency of its service. There is almost no human mediation. Everything is automatic, almost instantaneous. However, a massive economic and political structure exists behind of all those mechanical operations. A structure that puts pressure on publishing houses in order to maximize Amazon's profits from its products, just as it does on skateboard manufacturers or frozen-pizza producers. A macro-structure determining visibility, access, and influence is shaping our future.

IV   BECAUSE I DON'T WANT TO BE AN ACCOMPLICE TO A NEW EMPIRE

There are no booksellers on Amazon. Human book recommendations were eliminated because they were understood to be inefficient and because they torpedoed speed, the only value the company recognizes. Recommendations are now in the hands of an algorithm. An algorithm represents the height of fluidity. The machine transforms the customer into the prescriber. *Customers who bought this product also bought.* Self-publishing puts the process in the hands of the producer. Amazon eliminates intermediaries or makes them invisible as if they were so many robots. The company is like an ordering machine. It wants to be so streamlined as to seem invisible. Eliminating dispatch costs and haggling with clients means it gets the lowest possible price for the individual customer. Amazon seems cheap. Very cheap. But we now know that cheap means expensive in the long term. Very expensive. Because that invisibility is mere camouflage: everything is so quick and streamlined that there seems to be no middleman. But there is, and you pay for it with money and data.

Order, items, price, and dispatch: individual processes dissolve in the flow's non-material logic. For Jeff Bezos—as for Google or Facebook—pixels and links have a material correlative: the world of things can work like the world of bytes. The three companies share an imperialist desire to conquer the planet by defending unlimited access to information, communication, and consumer goods while forcing their employees, and their publishing partners, to sign contracts with confidentiality clauses, hatching complex tax-avoidance strategies in the countries where they are based, and constructing a parallel, transversal global state, with its own rules and laws, its own bureaucracy and hierarchy, and its own police. And with its own intelligence services and its own ultra-secret laboratories. Google X, the research and development centre for that company's future projects (from 2015 called Company X), is in a location not far from the firm's central headquarters that for a long time remained undisclosed. Its five-star plan has now become a network of stratospheric balloons called Project Loon that will bring billions of people around the world online, many for the first time. A parallel project is Amazon Prime Air, the company's new distribution network, which relies on 25-kilogram hybrid drones that are half-airplane, half-helicopter. In 2018, the US Federal Aviation Administration changed its regulations to facilitate the use of drones for commercial purposes and to make it easy to qualify for a drone-pilot certificate. Long live lobbying! Let our skies fill with robotic distributors of Oreos, cuddly toy dogs, skateboards, toasters, rubber ducks and... books.

Unlike Facebook and Google, who've to wrestle with the possibility that your name and data may be false, and who do all they can to get your phone number because they failed to request it when you originally opened your account, Amazon, from the very start, has had all your data: real, physical, and legal. Even your credit card number. The company may not have as much access to your emotional and intellectual profile as Google or Facebook, but it knows almost everything about what you read, eat, or like to give as presents. It's simple enough to deduce the state of your heart or brain from the goods you buy. Amazon's empire was born from items that enjoy the most cultural prestige: books. It built the world's biggest hypermarket behind a huge smokescreen shaped like a library.

V BECAUSE I DON'T WANT THEM TO SPY ON ME WHILE I AM READING

In the beginning was a single piece of data.

In 1994, Jeff Bezos read that the World Wide Web was growing at a monthly rate of 2,300 percent. So he left his Wall Street job, moved to Seattle, and decided to start selling books on the internet.

Ever since, the data has been multiplying, piling up organically like a monster with tentacles, a storm cloud, or a second skin: we have been turning into data. We leave it behind us in thousands of everyday operations that trace our fingerprints on the internet. Our cell phones send it out. We are constantly delineating our autobiography with our every act or tap on our keyboards.

On World Book Day in 2018, Amazon revealed what the most frequently underlined sentences on their Kindle platform were. If you read on your device, the company can find out everything about your reading habits. On what page you gave up on a book. Which pages you finished. How fast you read. What you underline. The great advantage of a print book isn't its portability, durability, autonomy, or even reading's close relationship with the memorization and learning processes, but the fact that it is permanently disconnected.

When you read a print book, the energy and data you release through your eyes and fingers belong only to you. Big Brother can't spy on you. Nobody can take that experience away or analyze and interpret it: it is yours alone.

That's why Amazon launched its global campaign, the "Kindle Reading Fund," ostensibly to encourage reading in poor countries, but in reality to accustom a new generation of consumers to read on screen, and to have the ability to study them and to get all five continents on its database. That's why the Planeta Group—a multimedia corporation that welds together more than a hundred companies, making it the sixth biggest communications group in the world—is investing in business schools, academies, and university institutions: because it wants to maintain high levels of literacy to ensure future sales of the novels that win the Planeta Prize. We'll see who wins out.

More specifically, let's see if we all win.

VI   BECAUSE I DEFEND BEING SLOW
YET QUICK, AND RELATIVELY CLOSE

Our moment has come.

Amazon appropriated our books. We will appropriate Amazon's logic.

First, by convincing readers of the need to keep time on hold. Desire cannot be fulfilled immediately, because it then ceases to be desire, and becomes nothing at all. Desire should last. I must go to the bookshop; look for the book; find it; leaf through it; decide if the desire was warranted; perhaps abandon the book and nourish the desire for another; until I find it; or not; it wasn't there; I order it; it will come in twenty-four hours; or in seventy-two; I'll be able to give it a glance; I'll finally buy it; perhaps I'll read it, perhaps I won't; perhaps I'll let my desire go cold for a few days, weeks, months, or years; it will be there, in the right place on the right shelf; and I will always remember in which bookshop I bought it and why.

Because a bookshop gives you a memory of your purchase. If you buy on Amazon, on the other hand, the experience is the same as the one before and after it. The aura around each book you read becomes diffuse and blurred.

Once we have tamed time and desire, perhaps the moment will come when we go one step further and put a bit of everything on the shelves. Let's not be afraid of diversity—it's what makes us human. Let there be coffee and wine in our bookshops.

Let there be bottles of Argentinian wine next to the complete works of Borges or Eterna Cadencia or Lucrecia Martel, Gotan Project CDs, Mercedes Sosa albums on vinyl, Martín Caparrós's *Hunger*, and three Carlos Gardel biographies (even though he wasn't Argentinian).

Or, better still, let's forget national categories as we have forgotten Aristotelian strictures. Unities of time or space no longer exist. In the twenty-first century, frontiers make no sense. Let's organize the shelves according to subject, let's mix up books and comics, DVDs and CDs, games and maps. Let's appropriate the same mix that exists in Amazon warehouses, but create meaning out of it. Itineraries of reading and travel. Because we might depend on screens, but we aren't robots. And we need everyday bookshops so they can continue mapping all the distant things that allow us to situate ourselves in the world.

VII BECAUSE I'M NOT INGENUOUS

No: I'm not.

I'm not ingenuous. I watch Amazon series. I buy books I can't get in any other way from iberlibro.com, which is owned by Abebooks.com, which Amazon bought in 2008. I constantly look for information on Google. And I am constantly giving my data, spruced up in one way or another, to Facebook as well.

I know they are the three tenors of globalization.

I know theirs is the music of the world.

But I believe in necessary, minimal resistance. In the preservation of certain rituals. In conversation, this is the art of time; in desire, this is time turned into art. Walking from my house to a bookshop, I whistle melodies that only I hear, that belong to nobody else.

I always buy books that aren't out of print in independent, physical bookshops, ones I feel a bond with.

Which is what I did the other day. I went to Nollegiu ("Don't read!"), my neighbourhood bookshop, and bought *On the City*, by the architect and thinker Rem Koolhas. And while I was drinking a cup of coffee, right there, I read: "Sometimes an ancient, unique city, like Barcelona, when it over-simplifies its identity, becomes Generic." Transparent, he adds. Interchangeable: "like a logo."

The book, by the way, was published by Gustavo Gili in this same city, when its head office was not what it is now.

The Best Bookshops in the World Aren't the Ones You Think They Are

Mark Rubbo, director of the seven branches of Readings bookshops in Melbourne, Australia, tells me they've been selling canvas bags emblazoned with the image of the original book shop's façade for over twenty years, but that it was only in 2016 they adopted the slogan "Shop local. Love your community," because "that was when Amazon came to Australia."

Nobody would think of walking through Melbourne with an Amazon T-shirt, whereas Readings bags are very visible in the centre of this cosmopolitan city. In recent years, the readers most aware of this new paradigm have made bookshops part of their identity. Bookshops are now wearable, photogenic, and sexy.

The global crisis coincided with the explosion of digital media that have made "best of" lists viral. Pinterest and Instagram (both launched in 2010) have popularized bookporn. Although the net is full of lists of the most beautiful, most famous, most important bookshops in the world, the truth is that the canon it has imposed lacks rigour, with each list copying another, and where the only criteria are a shop's previous number of citations and how photogenic they are.

Starting in 2016, however, more serious criteria have emerged for determining the planet's key bookshops. I am referring to the London Book Fair's Bookstore of the Year Award.

"I wasn't in London, but a couple of colleagues from the bookshop did go to the ceremony where the winner was announced," Rubbo tells me. They called him in the early hours: "It was the most exciting moment in my entire professional career." Readings had been chosen as the world's best bookshop.

What's more, Readings hadn't put itself forward with photos or numbers of followers on social media, but rather with data about their thirty-five years of activity, supporting local writers (through frequent book launches and a scholarship programme with the neighbouring Wheeler Centre), and working with the city (Readings Kids, Readings's beautiful children's and YA speciality shop, features a jungle mural by children's book illustrator Marc Martin that invites young patrons to come in and get lost).

Shakespeare and Company was awarded the prize in 2017. And in 2018 the distinction went to The English Bookshop in the legendary Swedish city of Uppsala. If we add the seven runners-up to those three, we would possibly have a list of the ten best bookshops in the world: Hoepli (Italy), Rahva Raamat (Estonia), Sanlian Bookhouse (China), Exclusive Books (South Africa), Time Out Bookstore (New Zealand), Cărtureşti Carusel (Romania), and Timbooktoo (Gambia). However, at least two issues make this list questionable. On the one hand, the fact that all three prize winners sell books in English. On the other, that not a single shop from the Hispanic world figures in the list. Even so, it is undoubtedly the most reliable selection we have at the moment.

"That recognition had wide coverage in the media," Rubbo says. But, although tourists from other Australian cities or even from Europe drop in now and then, attracted by the prize, "what's crucial to us is that, ever since, the bookshop has been held in even higher esteem by our own customers."

Photos of Readings may not have gone viral online—on websites, Pinterest, or Instagram. But images of their books, launches, and booksellers have certainly gone viral in the minds of Melbourne's readers. And that's what really matters.

Journey to the End of the Light

～ WALKING AROUND LONDON WITH IAIN SINCLAIR

> Repeated walks, circuits, attempts to navigate—
> to get to the heart of the labyrinth—proved frustrating.
> There was no centre.
>
> —IAIN SINCLAIR, *Lights Out for the Territory*

I   HOME

Iain Sinclair has just discovered that he owns an original photo by William S. Burroughs. We are in the kitchen of his house on Albion Road, in the heart of Hackney, a district he knows like the back of his hand and the soles of his feet; an observatory on the margins from which he has mapped and interpreted both the magical, ritualistic London of visionary poets and the Plague Years as well as the frenetic, multi-cultural London of motorways, tube-lines, and take-outs. Sitting behind his whitewood table he looks the picture of a retired Englishman, with his garden and grey squirrel out back (which right then jumps, climbs, and disappears). Yet whenever he gets up to look for a book, Sinclair's tall, sinewy body has the vitality of someone who walks seriously every day of the year, regardless the threat of rain, thunder, snow, or even terrorist attacks in this post-Olympic city in which thousands of cranes aim tensely at the sky as if, Ballard-like, they were crying out for an airplane to crash. He's just come back for the nth time holding a book. He opens it. And there it is.

"The photo was in this book," he says, showing it to me, "Brion Gysin dedicated it to me—we shared a publisher—and I found it because this year was his centenary, and they asked me for a cut-up based on the *Times* of the day of his birth and 19 January this year." When he saw the image, Sinclair remembered selling a suitcase full of original photos by Burroughs when he was working as a bookseller. One of them, having gotten trapped between the book's pages, has just resurfaced. In it, Burroughs appears with Gysin, a musician who was one of the many who helped create the orientalist image of Tangier as a city of extremes. Gysin was the inventor of the Dreamachine, a pioneer of computer-generated poetry, and the owner of a restaurant that was above all a psychedelic, social space. The composition of the black-and-white image recalls Velázquez's *Las Meninas*: the interplay of windows and mirrors creating repetitions of photographer and photographed. Maybe the photograph—with its ambiguous split image—is actually speaking to the origins of the "cut-up," a literary technique Gysin adapted, unawares, from previous avant-garde practice, and to which Burroughs gave form in some of the twentieth century's wildest, most emblematic novels.

"I started by selling some books I had sitting on pavements in Camden, and I'd soon inspired a market, two days a week. The headquarters, we might say, was here at home," he tells me. "I sold to bibliophiles from all over the world. I sold Burroughs's suitcase, which contained a huge collage, with lots of linked images, to an American." He bought his house forty years ago, for next to nothing. It is now worth two million pounds. He continues, "When it was being built, we found some strange relics. Apparently there used to be an old brickworks here." It was the base for his bookshop and publishing house: he still keeps remnants from that era in a room stuffed with boxes and junk, which I see as we leave the house. It is an archive waiting to be revealed. A psychogeography that was a network of walks. One day it will map not only London, but also various repercussions of international counter-culture.

ii A STROLL

In the doorway to his house he tells me that every walk he takes is a story, and that he cannot stroll without going off on a tangent. So we immediately abandon Albion Road and slip along unglamorous side streets with blocks of council flats where carpets and scarves, printed with images of Indian gods, elephants in lotus position, and faded friezes, hang. He is constantly reading walls, place names, and advertisements. "They drove out the legitimate inhabitants of this area, demolished their proletarian houses, and built those blocks that are blind to their murderous origins, and have no roots in this area," he says. He urges me to look at the posters advertising house sales: photos of the nearby train station; private, interior gardens; everything that radically separates them out from the district, from the territory. "They are commercially attractive because they are quite out of the way yet well connected, because they allow you to make a quick exit from here."

He can't take a step without reading the surface and the depths. He once walked with a diviner through Hackney looking for the course of a lost river, waters William Blake described in "Jerusalem." He found them. The branch shook. The energy is still flowing, despite the weight of their exile. One can feel it: it radiates from Iain Sinclair's feet, rises up his legs, infects you like hysterical laughter, as if the swaying movements of a single individual could counter the official discourse of an entire megalomaniac city.

In the 1995 film *Smoke*, a character takes a photo every day at the same time on the same Brooklyn street corner, recording the lives, times, and deaths of its inhabitants and quotidian passers-by. Sinclair, similarly, goes for a walk every morning around his neighbourhood, around London Fields, repeating millimetre by millimetre the same route, before starting work: "It keeps me in good shape, now I'm past seventy, and lets me savour the day's weather, and observe the small changes in that part of the city." For years he saw the same man with the same dog on the same bench in the same park. One day, he wasn't there. Nor the next. Soon after, someone put a plaque there to commemorate him. Sinclair's afternoon walk, however, is always different. Sometimes it finishes far away, and he returns by train. Other times, he gets lost: "It's impossible really to get to know London, I know some of its parts quite well, but the whole is... impossible."

The canal is beautiful in the evening light: dense, heavy clouds are reflected in its lapping waters. A couple of boats are moored there. We walk a few metres along the towpath, but after crossing the canal by New Road, we take a side street: "For decades I walked along the towpath, but it's out of the question now because you have to fight the cyclists and skaters." Like most cities in the Old World, London has idealized wheels without engines, with lanes for bicycles and campaigns to promote non-polluting transport, but has forgotten pedestrians. Determined to walk, Sinclair has challenged the logic of vehicular transport: in *Lights Out for the Territory* he invented nine routes for walkers to search out the city's hidden patterns; in *London Orbital* he walked along the edge of the M25, an urban highway going nowhere, a crazy loop, trawling for the remains of vanished villages and lives severed by speed and asphalt Scalextric, and in *London Overground* he walked fifty-six kilometres in one day, going to each of the different stops on the overland train's orange line.

"I made three excursions to prepare the hike for *London Overground*, that takes a single day, when I was accompanied by John Rogers the filmmaker," he tells me as we go down the stairs of Old Street Station, "but then we did it in reverse, because he had an accident, a horrific motorbike accident, and wanted to exorcize the pain with a nighttime stroll." And walking by night seemed a completely different phenomenon to daytime: "By day you stop at a café, you go into a bookshop, you buy a book, you sit on a bench, there are always people more or less around; by night, on the contrary, everything is quiet, sometimes dead, it's like sailing across a dreaming city."

After passing a florist's and a crêperie in the station's underground passageways, we come to Camden Lock Books, whose owner was one of the booksellers on Camden Passage from the good old days. While Sinclair buys the recent English edition of *The Unknown University* by Roberto Bolaño, I leaf through a short monograph on *Crash*, the David Cronenberg film based on a book by J. G. Ballard. Sinclair, Ballard, and Michael Moorcock are the contemporary metropolis' great narrators. While Martin Amis and his cronies narrate London from a literary realist perspective with modernist touches, counter-cultural writers like Ballard, Moorcock, Alan Moore, and Sinclair himself do so with an insane mix of all manner of styles and languages. Sinclair's projects almost always create a dialogue between visionary psychogeographic literature and documentary film. Ballard, likewise, has recourse to science fiction and forensic science. Moorcock is renowned for his magic demon sword sagas, but London is also a constant presence in his narratives, as in *Mother London* (where the city is recounted by psychologically disturbed patients) or the Cornelius series (which is set in a multiverse, but frequently visits districts like Notting Hill Gate or Ladbroke Grove). Moore revolutionized superhero comics and created some of the first serialized graphic novels, a form he took to extreme narrative ends in his masterpiece, *From Hell* (illustrated by Eddie Campbell), an exploration of the city in Jack the Ripper's time based on one of Sinclair's seminal essays, "Nicholas Hawksmoor, his churches," from *Lud Heat, A Book of the Dead Hamlets*. Moore also produced exhibitions and installations that broke down the boundaries between literature, film, video art, comics, and performance.

We leave the shop, weighed down by books, and reach our destination via City Road: Bunhill Fields. Sinclair tells me that the cemetery has ceased to be a secret place since the neighbourhood's recent gentrification. There are mothers taking their children for a walk, executives with their cell phones, girls with their dogs, and skateboarding adolescents... But no tourists. It's not on any circuit. It's as if tourism were punishing Daniel

Defoe and William Blake in the same way their contemporaries did: banishing them for not belonging to established religion. "Nobody notices Defoe's monolith, though there are always pilgrims who leave their offerings by Blake's gravestone, that is and isn't his grave, because we now know he was buried over there, under those trees, with eleven other people."

The afternoon's magnetic light filters through the trees' criss-crossing branches. A man is asleep on a bench, and five boys are larking around, their skateboards leaning on the wall and ground. Beyond them rises the belfry of a Hawksmoor church. Shakespeare had a theatre close to these graves. We are outside the city's ancient walls, in an area filled with brothels, hospitals, entertainment, and the non-conformist dead. Seven fat pigeons are resting on the tomb of John Bunyan, the pilgrim preacher. There is a medallion on the tomb's side. It shows him leaning on a stick, struggling to walk, literally crushed by the weight of his knapsack.

"I can identify with that image," says Sinclair, gripping his paper bag from Camden Lock Books. "I'm always walking weighed down by books." By literature. "Is this the city's magical centre?" I ask. "Not anymore. It has ceased to be that; now it's too public, too visible." "So what will the new centre be?" I ask. "I'm still looking... Perhaps I'll tell that in a future book."

III TAXI

"In my next book I will say goodbye to London: it will be called *London Final*," reveals Iain Sinclair on my last night in that canniballistic metropolis, as our taxi leaves the wealthy centre and penetrates the surrounding suburbs: "Then I will go to Peru and follow in the footsteps of my great-great grandfather, who went there to seek his fortune and wrote in a style similar to mine."

I didn't take notes on this conversation. We'd drunk a good deal of wine. Perhaps it wasn't his great-great grandfather, but his great-great-great grandfather. Perhaps I dreamed it. I'm not going to send him an email to check: he would never do that. But if it ever happens, that journey to South America will be a logical continuation of *American Smoke* (2013), the story of his road trip to the United States following in the footsteps of the Beat Generation. The book abandons Sinclair's usual territory, his infinite London, to visit the spaces where Jack Kerouac, Allen Ginsberg, William Burroughs, and Gregory Corso continued the visionary tradition of William Blake and the nomadism of John Bunyan. The New World routes where the Old World still had meaning.

I can't imagine him on a transatlantic flight. In Lima. In a rented car or a nighttime bus. The cordillera in the distance, like a curtain or a threat. I can imagine him wandering through Andean villages. He doesn't switch on his cell phone, he doesn't use GPS, he is never geolocated. I imagine him getting lost: travelling to the end of his own light. Osip Mandelstam says that Dante imagined a completely urban Inferno with alleys and stairs because it was his recreation of the city of Florence that sent him into exile. I imagine Sinclair wandering through indigenous markets and Inca ruins as if he were strolling through London, always going off on a tangent, always reading.

The World's Most Important Libraries Aren't the Ones You Think They Are

Helsinki's Oodi Library was inaugurated in 2018 and welcomed as the library of the future by the world's media. Designed by the ALA architects' studio, it's a striking building that houses one of those multimedia libraries that have come to be seen, across the five continents, as the best response to the question that agitates politicians in charge of culture: how to keep citizens coming back to shared, public book spaces?

Although it possesses a collection of one hundred thousand books and offers areas for silent reading, the Oodi puts a greater emphasis on its training, conversing, and meeting areas: the cafeteria, projection room, family space, restaurant, and lecture theatres and spaces of various sizes intended for informal encounters. Its prime attraction is the Citizens' Balcony, a large terrace with tables and chairs and spectacular views of the city.

All those features of Helsinki's Central Library were decided on democratically. As was the name, which means "ode." Even the budget is allocated on a participatory basis.

But none of that would have resulted in a global news story if the new library hadn't also been in Finland and weren't incredibly iconic. Because Nordic countries are synonymous—even in these times of deportations and institutional xenophobia—with social and pedagogical innovation, and the building housing this vanguard concept is beautiful and photogenic.

Like lists of the world's best bookshops, lists of libraries tend to mistake the spectacular for the excellent. Money can buy physical architecture, but it is harder to buy a structure of feeling. The best libraries in the world might not be housed in stunning buildings, have 3-D printers, or appear on the TV news, but they undoubtedly fulfil a purpose in their communities comparable to or better than these Nordic libraries. It is no accident that the clearest examples of this kind of institution are found in the Global South and are always less visible than in the Global North, even though they are projects that use reading, study, and art to fight discrimination, violence, and poverty.

Colombia's Mobile Public Library network—dubbed Mobile Libraries for Peace—uses modular structures that combine shelves filled with books and technological devices with reading and educational spaces. Twenty mobile libraries established in key parts of the country to encourage literacy as well as reconciliation for communities particularly fractured by civil war.

The National Library of Colombia's project, led by Director Consuelo Gaitán, adapts Philippe Starck's Libraries without Borders initiative to local needs. A secret intention of these hypermodern creations—described by their inventor as educational modules and mobile, pop-up multimedia centres—is to stimulate artistic ingenuity. In the rural municipality of Gallo, in Colombia's north, "peace librarian" Víctor Solís Camacho established two initiatives, the "literary canoe" and the "travelling mule library" (*muloteca*), which bring books, games, technology, and craft materials to vulnerable, post-conflict communities. Statistics show that literacy rates increase and crime rates and conflict decrease in areas with mobile libraries; adults have a safe place to converse and children to imagine futures, like going to university, that until very recently were completely denied to them.

In Honduras we can also find a model that is the opposite to emblematic buildings with a budget of millions. Thanks to children's library projects in the province of Lempira, initiated by the girl-centred Non-Governmental Organization Plan International, two hundred travelling backpacks are currently in circulation, which come from twenty-three school libraries and two public libraries that have revolutionized childhood by enabling kids to read stories systematically and create stories of their own. Reading and writing are also forms of what we call "empowerment."

The experiment has been so successful and so many pupils have found alternatives to violence or failure at school that in 2019 the Honduras National Congress debated a proposal that would replicate the experiment across the country. Meanwhile in Lempira five new libraries are being built and another ten have been approved. Because a library or travelling backpack are both invitations to read, and also stages for theatre, dance, puppets, mime and spoken word. They stimulate individual development and collective action.

Finland has the money, political will, and social dynamics that allow them to realize fantastic projects like Oodi. But that shouldn't eclipse the existence of another kind of project, more grass-roots and localized, that has to overcome lots of hurdles to achieve similar success.

In *La biblioteca fantasma* ("The Phantom Library"), a detailed, journalistic account of the systematic looting of the National Library of Peru over far too long a period, David Hidalgo analyzes one of the obstacles to this sort of project: corruption. It also offers a valuable profile of its excellent director, Ramón Mujica, who lost a quixotic battle to unmask the perpetrators and recover the stolen books.

In the course of singling out this bookish hero for praise, Hidalgo, investigative reporter and director of the online Peruvian newspaper *OjoPúblico*, reminds us of an indispensable truth: libraries are people, not buildings. From Alexandria onwards, libraries have no meaning without the commitment of each and every one of us—the turn of this century has seen some become dynamic performance stages. And they need more commitment now than ever.

In Lempira, children write reviews of the hundreds of books they read, and proudly display lists of the latter. Last year they published a book—edited by poets Salvador Madrid and Albany Flores—entitled *El árbol de los libros* (*The Book Tree*). Several of the stories are about reading and books. One is called "Superreader" and is signed by eleven-year-old Ariani Alcántara. It ends on this note: "only read to be happy."

Before and After Borges

> Borges's work is full of those rather dark, subaltern characters who follow like shadows the weft of a work or a more luminous character. Translators, exegetes, annotators of holy texts, interpreters, librarians, even the sidekicks of spivs and tough guys. Borges defines a true ethics of subordination [...] Being a footnote to someone else's life: doesn't that vocation as a parasite, at once annoying and admirable, nasty and radical, almost always prevail in the best of Borges's stories?
>
> —ALAN PAULS, *The Borges Factor*

I

Jorge Luis Borges's gravestone in the Cimetière des Rois in Geneva, which lies under the shade of a tree that only blossoms in alternate years, is located next to the grave of a prostitute. The epitaph for the author of "Pierre Menard, Author of the *Quixote*," a story whose protagonist is a fictional French writer, is kitsch: nobody understands his widow María Kodama's posthumous homage, whose incomprehensible Old English and Old Norse script, inscribed in type appropriate to a Nordic saga, sound as cacophonous as a Scottish bagpiper in the Gregorian chant of that sober, orderly landscape. Grass flourishes in the rectangle that has framed the corpse of Borges since his death in 1986. There are no messages, flowers, or stones, as there are, for example, around the Paris grave of Julio Cortázar. Conversely, the roses in the adjacent rectangle belonging to writer, painter, and prostitute Grisélidis Réal (1929–2005) are fresh.

Beyond their graves is an unfussy monument—a Swiss design—marking the remains of Robert Musil, who died in 1942 in Geneva, where he was sheltering from the Nazi tempest. A little further on, by the cemetery entrance, we find the grave of a Babel, who was perhaps a librarian. But the dead person next to the author of "The Lottery in Babylon" is a woman: an activist, a courageous woman, a cosmopolitan artist who was educated in Alexandria, Athens, and Zurich, a *poule de luxe* who always defended the marginalized, even at her funeral, which brought together dignitaries and the downtrodden, sex workers and millionaire watchmakers.

In the eyes of this cultural tourist, this enraptured traveller who spends his days in pursuit of literary topographies, there is a way to conceptually link Borges grave with Réal's via the vertex of another possible triangle: for here, too, lies buried Swiss philosopher Denis de Rougemont, who explained, like no one else, the ways we classify love in the West.

II

Borges is a parenthesis that lasted forty-five years: from 1930, when he published *Evaristo Carriego* and, soon after, met Adolfo Bioy Casares, to 1975, when his mother died and María Kodama became his personal secretary. Between those two dates he wrote all his masterpieces as an inhabitant of Buenos Aires and a memorable, iconoclastic reader with a deep knowledge of universal literature. Before and after Borges, on either side of that unrepeatable parenthesis, exists another Borges, who is less interesting from a literary perspective, but who is much, much happier. It is the Borges who, in 1914, arrived with his family in Geneva, where he studied for his secondary school certificate and became familiar with the avant garde; who then, in 1919, went to Palma de Mallorca, where he swam, stayed out late into the night, and signed the *ultraísta* manifesto; who returned to Mallorca sixty years later to visit Robert Graves, and who moved to Geneva in 1985 so he could die in Switzerland.

The canonical Borges is venerable and grandiose, increasingly abstract. He walks using a stick. He enters the dark or, once completely blind, disturbs us, like Tiresias, with his ironic visions. He writes stories that will stand the test of time, dictates poems and lectures, is translated and wins prizes. His world is Buenos Aires: he lives with his mother and their maid, Epifanía Uveda de Robledo (known, like his grandmother Fanny Haslam, as "Fanny"), he goes for strolls and dines with Bioy Casares, adores the tango, is a writer who reads and writes, more textually than emotionally. The other Borges, the first and the last, is passionate and physical. He writes letters, poems, and manifestos, and is still incapable of thinking about books. Having already written all the ones he could think up, he now thinks only of his *Complete Works*. As a young man, he travels with his family; as an old man, with María Kodama. He is happy, and unashamed to proclaim his happiness with life in his final destination, Geneva.

He was also happy in Mallorca: it's not difficult to imagine him there as you drive up the road to the villages of Valldemossa and Deià. The terraces and stone, the vertical walls and tormented trunks of olive trees: everything leads to the landscape he discovered so enthusiastically after living and studying in Switzerland as an adolescent. In a sad, metallic-grey Switzerland that, soon after he arrived, was transformed into an out-of-reach park by the First World War. He moved abruptly from Swiss geometry and affability to a cosmopolitan Mediterranean city just beginning to open to tourism, and from there to those terrestrial landscapes that at once charmed George Sand and provoked her visceral rejection, and which, conversely, enraptured Graves who, after staying silent during that whole encounter with Borges and Kodama, suddenly shouted from the doorstep: "You must come back! This is heaven!"

III

Mallorca's light offers a whimsical counter-point to Barcelona's darkness, through which you inevitably had to pass in times when there weren't so many airplanes: "a fortnight ago we left the Ciudad Condal (which is what the newspapers call Barcelona) to come and spend the summer in the Balearic Islands," Borges writes in *Cartas del fervor* ("Fevered Letters") on June 12, 1919. Irony distinguishes all the Borges we call *Borges*. Two years later he will be much more cutting, and speak of Barcelona as "the dirty, rectangular city."

The journey was his father's eccentric idea, he tells his close friend Maurice Abramowicz, and they meet in Palma de Mallorca, a city that is both beautiful and monotonous. Borges quotes from an exchange with a stranger when they talk about Switzerland, which he says has everything, "the city is so beautiful with its lake and the Rhône and…" He obviously idealized his life in Switzerland, which he now misses; and that's why day-to-day life in Mallorca palls. In the morning he catches the tram to Portopí to go swimming in the sea; in the afternoon he has classes with a priest; at night he reads in the Foreigners' Circle (say, Pío Baroja, and enthusiastically, because it's only in Barcelona that he slowly, then programmatically, decides to distance himself from Spanish literature and, finally, reject it.).

Portopí is now a large shopping centre. On the other side of the water, only a faint memory of the old port and its fishermen remains. To avoid the massive tourist invasion, you need to go a little further on, to Ses Illetes, a secluded military zone. The waters are transparent, almost saltless, and a very gentle blue. There are a few bourgeois mansions, and white sand straight from a picture-postcard. Here it's possible to imagine a young Borges, who had learned to swim in the Paraná and the Rhône, athletically flexing his muscles with each stroke taken under a blistering sun.

He gradually came to feel part of the city and the island, thanks to his conversations and friendship with Jacobo Sureda, a TB sufferer, with whom he shared a liking for the avant garde, and with whom he also discovered the pleasures of the night and of alcohol. In 1920 he said: "Mallorca is a place resembling happiness, a suitable place to feel content, a suitable backcloth to bliss and I—like so many islanders and foreigners—have never possessed that wealth of happiness one must have within oneself to feel oneself a worthy (and not shamefaced) spectator of so much limpid beauty."

He appears in photos wearing a youthful suit and tie, with his slightly greased hair combed back.

IV

There is an antiquarian bookshop on the Grande Rue with volumes I would love to own: first editions of works by the Situationist International, of Kerouac and Debord. There are also books from the eighteenth and nineteenth centuries. A woman's voice shouts at me from the back of the cave: "No photos!" After apologizing, I ask this plump woman in her sixties, who pushes up the spectacles that are about to fall off the end of her nose, whether Borges bought books there. She says he didn't. I don't believe her. Nor does she believe me when I say I didn't know photography wasn't permitted. We're even.

An hour later, when, after walking down the hill that is the historic centre and discovering the huge chess boards in the Parc des Bastions, I think of her again: our draw. Did Borges ever see those pawns, horses, or the two kings surrounded by sixty-four black and white squares? Did he know that one of his favourite symbols was there in three dimensions, a five-minute walk from his house? The latter is fifty metres from the bookshop, a side plaque (the street is full of plaques on façades commemorating names and dates of struggles for religious freedom and civil rights that nobody remembers today) recalling that Borges lived here. The quotation is from *Atlas*, the book he wrote with María Kodama, his testament written by four hands: "Of all the world's cities," the inscription notes, "I always think of Geneva as the one that most favours happiness." The quotation is reminiscent of another by Roberto Bolaño, from his address "Town Crier of Blanes," which appears in several corners of Blanes, Catalonia, where he lived for two decades until his death. One must look for grand statements in minor texts, the footnotes to those that really matter.

The adolescent Borges was introduced to the classics of French literature, books by Victor Hugo, Baudelaire, or Flaubert, by a mobile library in this city. It was Abramowicz who introduced him to Arthur Rimbaud. The Borges family lived on the Rue Malagnou (Marcos-Ricardo Barnatán relates in *Borges: Biografía total* that the street is now named after the distinguished Swiss painter Ferdinand Hodler) at number 17, "in the first-floor apartment with four windows that looked over the street, from 24 April 1914 to 6 June 1918," years when Borges studied at the Collège Calvin. The school's main subject was Latin, but almost everything was taught in French.

The family had gone to Switzerland after Borges's father experienced the first symptoms of the blindness that would force him to take early retirement, and which anticipated Borges' own blindness (there are men who assume their fathers' surnames as well as their lives). Curiously, despite the war, they crossed the Alps in 1915 and visited Verona and Venice. In his "Autobiographical Essay," where friendship finds pride of place, Borges recalls: "My best friends were of Polish-Jewish extraction: Simon Jichlinski and Maurice Abramowicz. One became a lawyer and the other a doctor. I taught them to play cards, but they learned so quickly and so well that they left me without a cent at the end of our first game."

I am fascinated by that journey taken in the middle of the First World War: that unexpected tourism. I can't find any mention of it in the biographies, though they all mention that Borges's sister Norah started to dream in French.

V

"We went to Mallorca because it was beautiful, cheap and there were hardly any tourists apart from us," continues Borges in his memoirs. "We lived there for almost a year, in Palma and in Valldemosa, a village on the top of hills." He continued to study Latin with a priest who had never felt tempted to read a novel, while his father wrote *El caudillo* ("The Strongman"), a worthwhile novel that forms part of the obsession with that male authoritarian figure and emblem of power we find in Latin American literature, from Domingo Faustino Sarmiento's *Facundo* to Mario Vargas Llosa's *The Feast of the Goat*, via Juan Rulfo's *Pedro Páramo* and so many others. Borges' father had five hundred copies printed in Mallorca, which he took on the boat back to Buenos Aires. Before he died, he asked his son to re-write it one day and clean up the inflated language.

He never did.

The letters from that period reveal how Borges followed the cultural debates in Europe from the island. In Republican salons it was common to discuss the theories of Einstein. With Sureda they continued their *ultraísta* plotting. Borges even found a barber who read Baroja, Huysmans, and Baroness Bertha von Suttner. When it was almost time to leave, he confessed he was sad about the return to Buenos Aires: "I'm collecting from here and there information about that peculiar country."

After leaving the Mediterranean, he never again saw Jacobo Sureda, who died in 1935, but he did meet up again with Jichlinski and Abramowicz in Geneva at the beginning of the sixties. They were so grizzled from old age he almost failed to recognize those "grey-heads," as he writes in his "Autobiographical Essay."

He doesn't mention his own blindness.

VI

The alphabets on Egyptian papyrus, in old Korans, in the Gutenberg Bible, in the very beautiful Japanese manuscripts known as pillow books, in the portrait of Dante attributed to Botticelli in first editions of *The Divine Comedy*, in Shakespeare's tragedies and in *Don Quixote*, all follow one another as if they were pages of a single book, a single textual history of humanity that you can read, walking under a subdued light, at the Martin Bodmer Foundation in Geneva. It is a subtle, intimate experience.

After a display with the Shakespeare and Company edition of *Ulysses* and a passing mention of its neighbour Musil (the third volume of *Man Without Qualities* was published in Lausanne, in 1943), as undisputed classics, Borges has a glass case all to himself in this museum of writing and books. The institution's official outlook is that literature, both Western and Eastern, ends with him: an ancient history that begins with the beautiful chaos of myth and ends with the perfection of the logos. The manuscript of "The South," from 1953, is on display, as are the first editions of *Ficciones* (Sur, 1944), *The Aleph* (Losada, 1949), and *The Book of Sand* (Emecé, 1975). There are some other manuscripts, and finally, in a revolving carousel that allows visitors to see the author's handwritten pages from both sides, the original version of "Tlön, Uqbar, Orbis Tertius" from 1940.

That glass case on the outskirts of Geneva, with its views of the lake and city, is Borges's true mausoleum, not the kitsch grave I visited this morning. A dynamic, classic, sober mausoleum like the Pléiade edition of his complete works. It is, with its gentle candlelight, a respectful tribute. All traditions, all alphabets end here; like a weathervane or compass card, the world that turns here is a tale.

VII

We know, courtesy of María Kodama, that Borges was happy in Geneva and so decided to die in Switzerland. Bioy Casares wasn't so sure. As he wrote on page 1590 of his monumental *Borges*, on Friday, February 14, 1986: "Ferrari tells me he is worried by the total lack of news from Borges. He says Fanny is worried too. After a while he confesses that Fanny has told him that according to the new doctor Borges is in a clinic, probably in Geneva. The new doctor must have reluctantly authorized him to travel, warning that 'the cold in Europe won't do you any good.' Borges told him: 'I'm not at all well. I don't how it will turn out. It makes no difference where I die.'"

These words, dictated by the grief of a friend whose own relationship with Borges had been undermined by Borges's young lover, almost hint at a conspiracy.

Bioy Casares didn't manage to speak to him until May 12: "she gave me the phone and I spoke to María. I informed her of trivial matters concerning royalties (out of politeness, to avoid more painful matters). She said Borges wasn't very well, that his hearing was poor and that I should speak up when talking to him. I heard Borges's voice and asked him how he was. 'Only so so,' he replied. 'I'll never come back.' The line went dead. Silvina said: 'He was crying.' I think he was. I think he called to say goodbye."

The diary only continues for another five pages. He talks about Kodama. Bioy says she was Borges's true love. That he died with his love. But also that she was a strange woman. That she criticized Borges, kept a jealous eye on him, was impatient at his slowness, punished him with silences (a harsh punishment for a blind man who can't see the expression on the face of the person keeping quiet). "I think he could feel very lonely with Maria," his old friend says, adding: "According to Silvina, Borges went to Geneva and got married to show that he was independent, like a youngster who wants to be independent and does something silly." Bioy then concludes: "He travelled to show that he was independent and to avoid upsetting María."

According to Edwin Williamson in *Borges: A Life*, it was that same drive to be independent from his family that led Borges to include pornographic allusions to brothels, alcohol, and gambling in his letters of farewell sent to Mallorca, sixty-five years earlier. Borges, the monument, the genius, the author of masterpieces all lived between parentheses his mother sustained like the Pillars of Hercules. "Strangely, it was in a brothel where the young Borges had a hint of the possible reconciliation of his inner conflicts," writes Williamson. Apparently, during his visits to Casa Elena in Palma, he established a curious friendship with a prostitute by the name of Luz, a relationship that granted the nervous, hypersensitive youth a sense of what a natural relationship with a woman might be like.

In the absence of love, he gave himself up to friendship. Jichlinski, Abramowicz, and Sureda were the young swimmer and avant-garde poet's best friends. Bioy Casares was the best friend of the ironic genius, of the Borges that matters. It fell to María Kodama to be his best friend at the end.

The last doctor who attended to him on his death bed was Jichlinski's son.

The footnotes fade like tears in the rain. What remain are the works. Great books like Casares's *The Invention of Morel*, which remind us that we are readers of words and passions and relationships and texts that produced holograms that increasingly look like desert islands.

Dear Mother,

Yesterday in the penumbra of a vast library, a private, almost mysterious ceremony took place. Some affable gentlemen made me a member of the National Institute of Arts and Letters. I was thinking about you all the time.

J.L.B., postcard from New York, March 26, 1971

I Dismantle My Library

I THE FIRST LIBRARY

I was thirteen and wanted to work. Someone told me that you could get paid to referee basketball games and where to go to find out about such weekend employment. I needed income to bolster my collections of stamps and Sherlock Holmes novels. I vaguely remember going to an office full of adolescents queueing in front of a young man who looked every inch an administrator. When my turn came, he asked me if I had any experience and I lied. I left that place with details of a game that would be played two days later, and the promise of 700 pesetas in cash. Nowadays, if a thirteen-year-old wants to research something he's ignorant about, he'll go to YouTube. That same afternoon I bought a whistle in a sports shop and went to the library.

I wasn't at all enlightened by the two books I found about the rules of basketball, one of which had illustrations, despite my notes and little diagrams, and my Friday afternoon study sessions; but I was very lucky, and on Saturday morning the local coach explained from the sidelines the rudiments of a sport which, up to that point, I had practised with very little knowledge of its theory.

My practical training came from the street and the school playground. My other knowledge, the abstract kind, stood on the shelves of the Biblioteca Popular de la Caixa Laietana, the only library I had access to at the time in Mataró, the small city where I was brought up. I must have started going to its reading rooms at the start of primary school, in sixth or seventh grade. That's when I began to read systematically. I had the entire collection of *The Happy Hollisters* at home, and *Tintin*, *The Extraordinary Adventures of Massagran*, *Asterix and Obelix*, and *Alfred Hitchcock and the Three Investigators* at the library. Arthur Conan Doyle and Agatha Christie were devoured in both places. When my father began to work for the Readers' Circle in the afternoons, the first thing I did was buy the Hercule Poirot and Miss Marple novels I hadn't yet read. That's probably when my desire to own books began.

The Biblioteca Popular de la Caixa Laietana acted as a surrogate nursery. I don't think children today have to write as much as we did in the 1980s. Long, typed-out projects on Japan and the French Revolution, on bees and the different parts of flowers, projects that were a perfect excuse to *research* in the shelves of a library that seemed, then, infinite and boundless; much greater than my imagination, then anchored in my neighbourhood and still restricted to three television channels and the twenty-five books in my parents' tiny library. I did my homework, researched for a while, and still had time to read a whole comic or a couple of chapters of a novel in whatever detective series I happened to be enjoying. Some children behaved badly; I didn't. The twenty-five-year-old librarian, a pleasant, rather custodial type, who was tall, though not overly so, kept an eye on them, but not on me. I'd go to him when I needed to find a book I couldn't track down. I also began to hassle Carme, the other young librarian, who saved us from her older, pricklier colleagues, with clever-clever, bibliographical questions: "Any book on pollen that doesn't just repeat what all the encyclopedias say?"

I mentioned my parents' micro-library. "Twenty-five books," I said. I should explain that Spain's transition from dictatorship was led by the savings banks. Municipal governments, busy with speculation and urban development, delegated culture and social services to the banks. Mataró was a textbook case: most exhibitions, museums, and seniors' centres, as well as the only library in a city of a hundred thousand inhabitants, depended on the Laietana Savings Bank. At the beginning of this century, during my (now real) research into Bishop Josep Benet Serra for my book *Australia: A Journey*, Carme, who has since become an exceptional librarian in Mataró, opened the doors of the Mataró holdings to me. I wasn't then aware of that defining metaphor, the 2008 economic crisis hadn't yet revealed the emperor's nakedness: Mataró's document holdings, its historical memory, wasn't in the municipal archive, wasn't in the public library, but in the heart of the Laietana Saving Bank's *People*'s Library. During the Spanish transition to democracy, the so-called duty to look after culture was assumed by the savings banks without anyone ever challenging them; it only became evident when one of them published a book, which they sent to all their customers as a free gift. I have one in my library that I inherited or purloined from my parents' house, Alexandre Cirici's *Picasso: His Life and Work*. The title page says: "A gift from the savings bank of Catalonia." It is the only institutional message. Although it's hard to credit, there is no prologue by a politician or banker.

43

There was no need to justify a gesture that was seen as *natural*. Over half of my parents' books were gifts from banks.

Years later, a childhood friend of my brother died in a traffic accident. Consumed by grief, his mother told mine that there was a woman in her support group who carried a newspaper cutting in her purse. She took it out. She read it aloud. Those words made her feel proud of her son, whom she'd so missed since the accident had killed him, his wife, and their two children. Those words helped her to live without her grandchildren, the children of a librarian disguised as a friendly policeman. Those words, partly erased by all those I've written since, were mine for a short while: now they belong to newspaper libraries that are gradually disappearing, because it's likely that, even for that mother, who will have partially overcome her grief, they are simply a memory. I'm not sure whether, in that obituary, I evoked those Saturday afternoons in a school playground, when I'd left the Mataró library for the library of the Pompeu Fabra University in Barcelona, where the friends of the not-so-young librarian and my friends and I played basketball together.

II   UNIVERSITIES

The other day I went down to the library of the university where I work to look for a copy of André Breton's *Nadja*, which I needed for a class, and which I couldn't find in my own library. There it was, in the same place it must have been in 1998, when I read all the surrealist books I could find, interested as I was in their theories about love (and my practice of it): *Mobile* by Michel Butor. But I didn't see it then. I did see it seven years later, in the University of Chicago Library, when I had the whole winter ahead of me to read. I sense that bookshops display the books in their possession in a seductive, almost obscene, manner because they want to sell them to you; conversely, libraries hide or at least camouflage them, as if they were content just to hoard. But it's also true that it's your gaze that scans the books' spines, that it's your attentiveness or whim that determines whether the titles and authors are revealed or go unnoticed.

The Pompeu Fabra University Library was very new when I started my first year in humanities. It was so young its sections didn't even have names. As a library matures, it begins to house donations, collections, archives, each bearing the name of a donor, a scholar, or someone retired or dead. In relation to a library, we associate the verb "to exhaust" with Borges. I am someone who exhausts bookshops and libraries; I love to spend hours looking at sections, shelf by shelf; the books, spine by spine. I have done this on rainy days in many of the world's cities. On snowy days, only in one: Chicago. I have never felt so lonely as in those weeks at the beginning of 2005. I came to spend twelve or thirteen hours in that enormous library. Before I discovered the interlibrary loan system that gives you access to any book in any library in the United States, I spent many hours in the Spanish literature section, in search of travel books and essay collections you can only find in that way, via the pre-digital google of meandering around a labyrinth of books. My Ariadne's thread: all those titles and pages, their secret disarray. Loneliness; there is no worse minotaur.

Using a neophyte library like the one at my university, Chicago's—and before that, the University of Barcelona's—alerted me to a key cultural concept: holdings. That possible memory of a particular state of culture and the world. That fragment you will never fully know of a whole that can never be reassembled. Holdings are often bottomless pits, places where unpublished manuscripts and the most important letters can exist without being seen (or worse, read) by anyone. At the pit bottom of the University of Chicago's history, or simply on the foundation stone of its book collection, we find the first of many names to come: William Rainey Harper. His erudition and pedagogical experiments reached the ears of Rockefeller, who promised him $600,000 to create a centre for higher education in the Midwest that could compete with Yale. In the end, $80 million came the University of Chicago's way, because, in addition to writing Greek and Hebrew textbooks, Harper was spinning strategies so that the poor, and those who worked full-time, could get access to higher education. He was an excellent manager. He created the university press that survives to this day. On the other hand, the William Rainey Harper Memorial Library was closed in 2009. The message on Librarything couldn't be starker:

> University of Chicago—William Rainey Harper Library
> Status: Defunct
> Type: Library
> Web site: www.lib.uchicago.edu/e/harper/
> Description: On June 12 2009, the William Rainey Harper
> Memorial Library was closed, and its collections trans-
> ferred to Regenstein Library.

Defunct library. The demise of a library as the final death of an individual who survived almost a century after his actual death. It makes you think there's no word more pretentious than *university*.

In one of his now forgotten articles about literature, which I finally read the other day in the Humanities library of the university where I work, Michel Butor writes: "a library offers us the world, but offers us a fake world, sometimes there are cracks, and reality rebels against books, through our eyes, a few words or even certain books, something strange that points to us and triggers the feeling that we are shut in." I think he is right: a bookshop gives material form to the Platonic, capitalist idea of freedom, whereas a library is often more aristocratic and can sometimes be transformed "into a prison." In our homes, thanks to, or through the fault of, bookshops, we imitate the libraries we have visited from childhood and construct our own bookish topography. Butor says: "By adding books we try to re-construct the whole surface, so windows appear." In reality we add centimetres of thickness to the walls of our own labyrinth.

III   MY LIBRARY IS FALLING TO PIECES
BUT IT IS STILL MY MEMORY

Until now I had often been unable to find dispensable books, ones you could almost do without, on my own shelves; but the day I couldn't find *Nadja*, one of those novels I have regularly dipped into over more than ten years, like *Don Quixote*, *Heart of Darkness*, Julio Cortázar's *Hopscotch*, Thomas Mann's *The Magic Mountain*, or David Grossman's *See Under: Love*, I was forced to start worrying. In his famous essay "Unpacking My Library: A Talk about Book Collecting," urban nomad Walter Benjamin says that any collection oscillates between order and disorder. The like-minded Georges Perec sets out, in *Thoughts of Sorts*, an

47

unarguable principle: "A library that is orderly, becomes disorderly: it's the example I was given to explain entropy and I have verified it several times experimentally." I must admit that in the four-and-a-half years that have passed since I moved to a flat in the Barcelona Ensanche I have accumulated books, and the odd set of shelves, without reordering my library's overall structure. And now everything is horribly chaotic.

The world's logic is mimetic. Everything works by imitation. The originality of our personality is but a complex combination of options we have borrowed from various models over time. My library is a response to the void of my parents' house: there are traces of all the public libraries I've visited since childhood. The other day I came across some photocopied pages of Paul Bowles's diary, pages that bore the Caixa Laietana stamp. I also hoard the books I've bought from the University of Chicago Library, which periodically gets rid of books in a fleeting—weekend—conversion of the library into a second-hand bookshop. When I last moved house, I arranged my library by language tradition and remoteness of interest. I keep next to my desk books about literary theory, communication, travel, and the city. Two feet behind those books is Spanish literature, in alphabetical order. Opposite them, three or four feet away, world literature. You must walk to the adjacent room, the dining room, to access historical, film, and philosophical essays, biographies and dictionaries (made even more distant by their online versions). I keep comics and travel books in the passageway. And in the guest room, finally, Catalan literature, essays on love, my books on Paul Celan, several hundred Latin American chronicles, as well as two copies of each of the books I have written or contributed to. Logic and caprice intertwine in a library that has occupied different spaces as the number of books grows and visits to Ikea are made. The bookcases in the study are solid wood: my parents, who still believe in solidity, bought them with my money to house the prototype of this library when I went travelling in 2003. But the rest of the apartment is filled with Billy shelves bent under their load, and gradually coming apart as a result of my lack of dexterity, which condemned them to degeneration the moment I screwed them so poorly together; I may be a more or less competent reader, but I'm a hopeless DIYer. My childhood toys included a microscope, mineral and physics kits, as well as a toolbox: I hardly need to say I didn't end up specializing in carpentry or the sciences.

"Every collection is a theatre of memories, a dramatization and staging of individual and collective pasts, of a childhood remembered and a souvenir after death," Philipp Blom wrote in *To Have and to Hold: An Intimate History of Collectors and Collecting*, adding: "it is more than a symbolic presence: it is a transubstantiation." All those books that surround me every day allow me to feel near to myself—to what I was, to that reader who kept growing, changing, adding layers—and to the information and ideas they contain. Or that they only suggest. Or that they only hyperlink: many of my books are planets orbiting around thinkers, writers, and historical figures I don't know firsthand, but that are friends of friends, involuntary accomplices, shifting pieces in a complex system of potential knowledge.

Friends, acquaintances, future contacts. Those are the three labels around which I'm going to organize my library, I decide as I finish writing this essay, when we rearrange the house next month for happy, familial reasons. I will dismantle it in order to reinvent it. I shall place near me only those writers and books with which I enjoy a more or less close friendship. These will stay in (or will enter) the study. They'll surround me, as their memory already does, or that of their authors. I will keep acquaintances in the dining room, the ones I respect and feel fondly towards. Most of the books I haven't read, and that I don't know if I ever will, will be given away and sacrificed; those that remain, in the passageway, will await their turn, patiently, distantly, like people you don't know, whom you may never know.

Aby Warburg, founder of the twentieth century's most fascinating library, placed a single word over the entrance: "Mnemosyne." His books and prints moved and migrated according to dynamic relationships of affinity and sympathy, creating provisional collages and leaving it to readers to imagine the links between them. As far as he was concerned, a library's only reason to exist was as a place where one could stroll and wander. In the stroller's gaze, images and texts fired invisible arrows at each other: neuronal synopses: the electricity nourishing the history of form and art. "It's not merely a collection of books, but a collection of problems," said Toni Cassirer, the wife of German philosopher Ernst Cassirer, after paying it a visit: a library only has meaning if it soothes as much as it disturbs, if it resolves, but above all, poses riddles and challenges. Cohabiting with a personal library means that you're not surrendering, that you will always have fewer books read than books left to read, that books that keep company with one another are chains of meanings, mutating contexts, questions that change according to tone and response. A library must be heterodox: only the combining of diverse elements, of problematic relationships, can lead to original thought. Many of those who saw Warburg's library described it as a labyrinth.

In his introduction to *Warburg Continuatus: The Description of a Library*, Fernando Checa writes: "As a theatre and arena of the sciences, the Library is also a real 'theatre of memory.'" Which is what this essay has attempted to be. "There will never be a door," wrote Borges in a poem precisely entitled "Labyrinth," "You are inside / and the castle encompasses the universe / and has neither obverse nor reverse, neither external wall nor secret centre."

The Legendary Bookshops
of David B.

$\mathbf{B}$efore Walter Benjamin decided to write his huge, and unfin-
ished, *Arcades Project*, Louis Aragon published one of Benjamin's
inspirations: *Paris Peasant* (1926), a hypnotic book that counter-
points two highly significant spaces in the French capital in the
nineteenth century: passageways and parks. Like his companion
in alcoholic, poetic adventures, André Breton, Aragon strolls
through a Paris that floats, where every corner and door can lead
to a hallucination or a dream. Three very different writers are
among the heirs to that seminal work: Benjamin, narrator and
philosopher, or philosophical narrator; novelist and essayist
Georges Perec (the lists of police stations, tax and post offices
could well belong to the author of *Species of Spaces* [1974]); and
the graphic artist and scriptwriter David B. For when Aragon
describes in great detail the Passage de l'Opéra, he takes two
bookshops as his points of reference, one inside the passage and
one outside it: Rey and Flammarion. This could be the secret avant-
garde starting-point of *Incidents in the Night* (1999). Reinventing
surrealism. Reinventing Paris. And doing so by weaving vignettes,
digressions, and dreams via the connecting thread of bookshops.

This two-volume comic, which promises a sequel that will
probably never appear, because David B. is well known for

abandoning projects, begins with the combination of a dream and a bookshop. The hero, who is very like the author, dreams in 1993 of finding volumes two and three of a serial or magazine entitled *Incidents in the Night*, fantasy stories set at the turn of the nineteenth century. From that moment he begins a pathetic, oneiric, and epic search for the other volumes. A search that will lead him to cross paths with Azrael, the angel of death; with Enn, the ancient god of slaughter and oblivion; with a detective hardened by a thousand dirty tricks, whose archive hoards all the despicable events that have occurred in the city and the government; with a gang of criminals who hide and multiply; and, above all, with the most emblematic booksellers in Paris, because the key to his investigation lies in its bookshops: nodes of a network that give the city another meaning.

Incidents in the Night was preceded by two other volumes, which display a similar imagination, and are set in the years after the First World War and feature protagonists who originally appeared in *Reading the Ruins* (2001). These two installments in the *Black Paths* series make clear the author's interest in the historical avant garde and his investment in dream-states and the subconscious. He reconstructs Gabriele D'Annunzio's Dadaist adventures in Fiume and plants the seed that comes to fruition in his later work: in the final pages the protagonist, Lauriano, "was writing articles for *Incidents in the Night*, each time under a different pseudonym. He tried to appear as little as possible in all the events in his lifetime. He sharpened his senses on a search for signs of Never-Never Land." If these projects can be seen as two acts in the same brilliant theatrical drama, the colour in *Black Paths* (the work of colourist Hubert, using David B.'s originals) distances this work from pulp fiction and brings it close to the plastic arts in the era he describes and the artistic explosion that took place between the two world wars. *Incidents in the Night*, however, could only be in black and white, because, although the world it depicts is equally surreal, its paths are truly black, with no possibility for the love and happy ending of its predecessor.

The result of David B.'s comings and goings in that Paris of second-hand bookshops and criminal connections, of police departments and apartments where the most savage murders are committed, is even stranger than D'Annunzio's milieu in Fiume. It is a fascinating topography that contains as many elements from the city of surrealists and Oulipo as the pulp tradition of Eugène Sue's *The Mysteries of Paris* and the comic underground. Yet at the same time it is, above all, absolutely personal. Like *From Hell*, by Alan Moore and Eddie Campbell, which reveals a symbolic, secular London (which Moore extracts from the work of post-situationist Iain Sinclair, that dark sage of the metropolis, the obverse of the luminous Peter Ackroyd, the city's official biographer), *Incidents in the Night* forces us to look at the city in a new way; one that is mythological, mythographic, topsy-turvy, and dazzling. Beyond the story, pages, and Paris, the work beats with a timeless narrative of destruction. Digressions that relate various, post-Babylonian versions of the myth of the universal flood, the first genocide carried out by the gods, and the extinction of the huge prehistoric mammals—the first extinction carried out by human beings—carry the comic to stratospheric flights, even though they are descents into hell. Constant switching from adventures to philosophical reflection, from action set in slums to Kabbalistic connections, from the story of the detectives to mythological figures, make *Incidents in the Night* a masterpiece. In my opinion, it is the author's most important work.

David B.'s major works shift between reality and imagination, between realism and dreams. His best known title, *Epileptic* (1996), which is also a family tale based on the figure of his sick brother, is an artist's autobiography where one sees the genealogy of his vocation and craft, drawing on the huge artistic resources of his imagination to escape the crushing nature of reality via a myriad of mythological creations. His illustrations in *Best of Enemies: A History of US and Middle East Relations* (2012), a three-volume pop history written by Professor Jean-Pierre Filiu, are initially faithful to the text; as the series proceeds, however, they transmute by degree—and entirely in the second volume—eventually becoming the freest possible interpretation of the accompanying words. Pages and pages of interpretation. A torrential, symbolic visualization of the universe. I think we get the best of David B. when reality is the starting point, but not necessarily the destination, as in *Black Paths* or *Incidents in the Night*, because he translates whatever material he is working with—documents or dreams—into his own referential graphic universe; a universe that is more dreamlike than documentary.

All the works I have mentioned share a vision of a world rent by conflict. The criminal gangs in *Black Paths* or *Incidents in the Night*, with their confrontations and massacres; the dozens of skirmishes and wars between the United States and various Middle Eastern countries in *The Best of Enemies*, whose prologue connects these images of violence to "The Epic of Gilgamesh"; the author's family's confrontations with doctors, neighbours, and other individuals in *Epileptic*. This is also true in other, lesser titles like *False Faces: An Imagined Life of the Wig Gang*, written with Hervé Tanquerelle, which represents a universe of conflict between law and crime, order and chaos. *Black Paths*'s most blood-curdling vignettes of those struggles are represented by visceral etchings, inspired by painters like George Grosz, in which men are equated with dogs. Elsewhere, these representations take us to mythical drawings inspired by sacred texts and legends. Which means that, for David B., surrealism and the language of comics are merely vehicles for connections with the collective subconscious and its gallery of shapes and symbols, with the gods we have been killing, and with the violence of our own origins.

From Little Havana to Miamizuela

"In New York Spanish is a language of the kitchen, whereas in Miami it's the language of power," Pedro Medina tells me as we drive along Biscayne Boulevard. After reading *Warsaw*, a dirty novel populated by Miami Beach prostitutes and police, I was expecting a tough, tattooed guy riding a Harley Davidson. The man who turned up instead was a forty-one-year-old Peruvian in shades and a black polo shirt at the wheel of a grey Volkswagen Jetta who has spent most of his adult life here. In this pedestrian-free city, it seems reasonable enough for our interview to take place at fifty kilometres an hour.

"Miami is a place that's changing all the time," he declares. That's why what happened in *Miami Vice* in the 1980s isn't unusual. Through clothes, visual effects, and a new wave and techno soundtrack, Michael Mann's series invented a metropolis that didn't exist in reality. "But over time reality ended up looking like the series."

Sonny Crockett and Rico Tubbs's boss was Lieutenant Martin Castillo, who hailed from Cuban stock. Twenty years later, *Dexter* arrived and the police inspector changed genre but not origins: Maria LaGuerta also came from the island. Although the present mayor of Miami, Francis X. Suárez, is

59

the son of Cuban-born former mayor Xavier Suárez, the map of power is changing, as is the makeup of the journalistic and literary worlds.

When Medina arrived from Lima at the beginning of the century, the city was mainly Anglo-Saxon and Cuban: "I always point out the novel of that period, *Nieve sobre Miami* ('Snow over Miami') by Juan Carlos Castillón, because the noir genre was in the hands of Anglo writers and it was that book, written by an author from Barcelona who'd spent years in the Americas, which started the process of narrating Miami in our language."

Over the last ten years, this has been the aim of the Suburbano writers: to encourage journalism, fiction, and criticism written in Spanish through their digital newspaper portal and the publication of books. Books like *Viaje One Way: Antología de narradores de Miami*, edited by Medina and Hernán Vera (the project's other founder from Buenos Aires), which has become *the* reference book if you want to understand the literary transformation of this slowly sinking city. The platform, and Vera's literary workshop, can count on the support of over twenty writers who regularly meet up; a Latin American scene with authors like Peruvian Rossana Montoya Calvo, Argentinians Gabriel Goldberg and Gastón Virkel, or Venezuelan Camilo Pino. Although the young Legna Rodríguez Iglesias and veterans José Abreu Felippe and Antonio Orlando Rodríguez ensure a Cuban accent is still heard, it's no longer the accent that predominates in the books written here in the home of Peruvian Jaime Bayly, Argentinian Andrés Oppenheimer, or Mexican César Miguel Rondón.

These urban thoroughfares, island-like districts with their extremes of opulence and dire poverty, this tropical-scented, muggy heat and sinking city and every single hurricane: all are recounted in our language's every accent.

"Yo hablo perfecto inglés," a mixed-race girl says in perfect Spanish to a gentleman wearing a *guayabera*. Not one of the forty-three people currently in the Versailles Bakery—the most famous Cuban restaurant in the world, according to the sign, and it may be true—is speaking English. They're ordering *croquetas, empanadas gallegas, tortillas de pimiento, sándwich cubano*, cheesecake, *pastel tres leches, tartaleta de manzana* or *nueces*, which they wash down with fruit juice or a cortado with evaporated milk.

Ever since it opened in 1971, the Versailles has been an important rendez-vous point for Cuban exiles. Fidel Castro's death, on November 25, 2016, was celebrated euphorically here with music and rum. The floor is a green-white beehive of worn hexagon tiles. Rich Cubans no longer live around here, but come to meet their friends or to throw tea parties for their children. CIA agents and Cuban exiles conversed in hushed tones for decades in Little Havana, conspiring and plotting terrorist attacks. Several of those encounters probably took place around these very tables.

"Right now those meetings happen in El Doral, an area of Miami known as Doralzuela, plotting the end of Maduro," Medina tells me as he takes off his sunglasses. He continues: "In ten or fifteen years we'll be studying Venezuelan Miami the way we now study Cuban Miami."

We say goodbye after walking past cigar shops, salsa and mojito joints, and El Parque del Dominó, where old Cubans play as if they were robots, or attractions in a theme park of Cuban exile. "Now I'll take off my writer's gear and put on my office suit," Medina confesses as we shake hands: "I work in a Venezuelan bank."

It's forty minutes by Uber and almost half a century of Latin American history from Little Havana to Miamizuela: from 1959 to 1999, from the Cuban Revolution to the start of Comandante Hugo Chávez's presidency. "My dad's parents are Cuban and he was born in Cuba, but arrived in Venezuela at the age of three. He knew what a communist regime was like, and declared in the first year of the Chávez government that he wouldn't stay there, and came to the United States," says Verónica Ruiz del Vizo—who, at thirty-two years old, has a sparkle in her eye and 115,000 followers on Instagram. "He belongs to the first group of immigrants from Venezuela who arrived at the beginning of this century with lots of money and he bought houses in two areas, Weston and El Doral. He invested, set up businesses, but it wasn't a wave of immigration that caught the headlines."

Hers is the one that starts to make an impact in 2014. Protests, repression, and successive crises choke the Venezuelan air: thousands of students, professionals, journalists, and intellectuals started arriving in waves that continue to the present. Most settle in El Doral. And they've started to organize like a proper diaspora.

The director of Mashup, the digital-content managing agency that Verónica founded almost ten years ago, when still at university, is now one of the leading voices of that second massive migration from Latin America to Miami. One of the initiatives she is involved in is Dar Learning, an educational program in which several distinguished professionals, with over ten years of experience in their fields, give free online courses to help people in the process of migrating.

"What makes our literature different from Cuban literature," Verónica opines, "is that pop music and technology were never important to them but have been central for us. What makes our diaspora different from the Cuban one," she continues, "is that many of the first Venezuelans who arrived here had experience in the corporate world and found positions at the executive level, when they didn't open branches of their own businesses, and all us young people who arrived later had lots of experience in the modes of expression used on social media." Twitter, for example, is used by thousands of citizens from Caracas and other cities in the country to get penicillin or blood.

Through Facebook, Instagram, WhatsApp, or Twitter, immigrants from the cultural world have been able to link up and organize themselves at an unprecedented rate. El Paseo de las Artes, which shut down in El Doral, for example, has reopened in Wynwood with a great theatre and comedy program. Its venues are full every weekend. In the subculture of exile, George Harris has become a stand-up comedy star by making jokes about Nicolás Maduro, Diosdado Cabello, and even his own mother.

"This has led to an unexpected alliance between Colombian and Venezuelan immigrants, in theatres, art galleries, and handicrafts," adds this dynamic cultural leader. Even *arepas* have become a meeting point, chefs from both countries having reinvented them, via nouvelle cuisine, and put them on the menus of their restaurants. The centuries-old debate about who invented the *arepa* has finally come to a truce in Miami; let's hope that

Chilean and Peruvian immigrants can also find a way to agree on intellectual property rights for the pisco sour.

The most emblematic space of the Venezuelan community in El Doral over the last fifteen years is located in a gas station, this suburb having been an industrial area and dumping ground before the torrent of investments by new arrivals was unleashed. There are several trucks and a statue of Simón Bolívar in the Arepazo parking lot. At 1 p.m. on a Wednesday in September, all the tables are occupied except for three, which have a *reserved* card with Barça's crest on one side and Madrid's on the other. On the wall, under nine plasma televisions, is this *arepa* and *tequeño* restaurant's slogan ("The Venezuela of Yesteryear: How to Forget it") and several newspaper pages ("Liberation Day. 18 hours of frantic celebrations in Caracas because the dictator has fallen"). No doubt there will be loud celebrations here when Maduro meets his end.

There's only one cultural space in CityPlace Doral, a mixed-use complex that's ten minutes by Uber and ten years of Venezuelan diasporic history away. There are three-bedroomed apartments that cost $3,620 a month and restaurants and ice cream parlours on the ground floor. Cinébistro offers a menu of shots and Latino dishes and another of Hollywood films. *Ceviche* or *churrasco* with jalapeño pineapple margaritas before seeing, say, *Crazy Rich Asians*.

"Why don't you open a branch of Altamira in El Doral?" I ask Carlos Souki, owner of the only exclusively Spanish bookshop in Miami's Coral Gables. "Because we're not interested in simply focussing on Venezuelan readers, though that's what we are, and it's here, between Books and Books and Barnes and Noble, where readers of our language from the whole city come. That's why we were keen to be here."

In Caracas Souki and his wife, Susana, owned record shops, having discovered, in the 1980s, a public interested in English music that couldn't get what it wanted: "And here we discovered that there was also a public that wasn't happy, but in the opposite direction, one that was hungry for literature in Spanish, and that's why we import books from Spain, Mexico, Colombia, and, until not long ago, from Argentina. So all these people can have access to what they want." After going to the Liber Book Fair in Madrid and reaching agreements with the biggest publishing houses, they realized they could compete with Amazon, which doesn't enforce as aggressive a pricing policy in the United States as the one driving its sales in English, because it does business through third parties. "Amazon is the bogeyman, then," smiles Souki, pointing to wooden shelves bathed in green light, "but we have succeeded in ensuring that 80 percent of our titles are offered at a lower price than those from the name we cannot name."

Seventy percent of Miami's population speaks or understands Spanish. The Miami Book Fair organizes almost two hundred events a year with Spanish-American authors. But the market is very influenced by social and cultural pressure from the Anglo-Saxon world and Altamira has been struggling for two years to persuade Miami's inhabitants, accustomed to clock-watching their daily lives and buying on the internet, to come to the Miracle Mile and spend an afternoon among books.

"So you can get an idea what people's habits are like, even among Latinos, I can tell you that our best customer calls us every third Monday to give us a list of the books he wants three Mondays later, and sends us a cheque; we don't know him, he lives four blocks away, but we've never seen his face: one day we told him we could deliver the books personally, and he told us not to bother him: he preferred us to post them."

My Bookish Buenos Aires

∽ **AN INTERVIEW WITH
ALBERTO MANGUEL IN THE
NATIONAL LIBRARY OF ARGENTINA**

In Alberto Manguel's office as director of the National Library of Argentina, a poster for Dante's seventh centenary and a bust of the poet, a photograph of Jorge Luis Borges, a large blue and white flag, and a small green plastic dinosaur immediately catch my attention. "That was a present from my son," the Argentine-Canadian writer tells me. Bibliophile, cultural nomad, teacher, translator, editor, essayist, novelist, anthologist, critic, multilingual polymath, cultural facilitator, and, above all, reader: the layers of Manguel's seventy years are evoked in the gleaming eyes behind his glasses. "Because its name is Albertosaurus and its skeleton was found in the Canadian province of Alberta," he continues before sitting down in a large armchair. He offers me the other, and we start to talk.

*　*　*

We are in an institution that everyone links with Borges. How does your experience as director of the National Library help you to understand the master?

These are only two connected facts in that universal constellation where everything is connected. Borges was the symbolic director of the library; a universal director, a universal librarian who represented not just the National Library of Argentina, but the Library in all its facets. Now, naturally, the National Library, as an institution of stone and steel and paper and ink, implies extra-literary obligations, needs, and functions. Borges was a symbol of the literary, and literature is divided into a Before and an After Borges. One cannot write in Spanish or in any other language without feeling his presence, either consciously or unconsciously. Texts like "Pierre Menard..." change forever one's notion of what writing and reading mean. My mission is located in another, completely different field, that is administration pure and simple. I gave up my career as a writer and, to an extent, as a reader, when I took on the post of director of the National Library at the end of 2015, and became the person responsible for removing obstacles to the work of the eight-hundred-plus individuals who work here. Do you know *Café Müller*, the ballet by the great German choreographer Pina Bausch? Do you remember that it's about a woman who is dancing and another character who is removing the chairs from her path so she doesn't stumble? Well, I am that second person.

In With Borges, *your book of memoirs, you relate Borges's work as a librarian to yours as a bookseller, because he used to visit the bookshop*

where you worked after he left this library's previous headquarters. Apart
from meeting Borges, what else did that first experience as a bookseller
bring you?

I worked in the Pigmalion Bookshop, where we sold books in
English and German, when I was fifteen, sixteen, and seventeen.
I went to school in the afternoon. And Borges went there to
buy his books, and one day he asked me to go to his house
and read to him, as so many other people did. I already knew
that I wanted to live among books, I realized that the world
was revealed to me through books and that the world then
confirmed or provided an imperfect version of what books
had shown me. Borges taught me two basic lessons. The first
was not to worry about the expectations of the adult world,
which wanted me to be a doctor, engineer, or lawyer—I come
from a family of lawyers—and to accept my destiny among
books. The second concerns writing. Borges wanted me to read
him the stories he thought were almost perfect, particularly
by Kipling, but also by Chesterton and Stevenson, because he
wanted to revisit them before starting to write new stories of
his own. He had stopped writing when he became blind, and,
ten years later, in the mid-sixties, he decided to write again.
He wanted to see how they were put together. Let's remember
that for Borges there is an important word, a word the Anglo-
Saxons used to call a poet: the "maker." For Borges, writing was
manual work, a form of engineering; then he would dissect
the text, interrupting my reading after one or two sentences
to observe how words were combined, what words had been
chosen, what tense was being used, how one sentence was
reflected in the next. That second lesson, a lesson connected to

writing, was that one must be familiar with the art in order to write. The English have the word "craft" to denote the artisanry of a text. Until then I had believed literature was emotional, philosophical, and adventurous. Borges taught me to worry about how that text was constructed before thinking about the emotion I wanted to communicate. As if my relationship with people to that point had been through what they said, their physical appearance, and suddenly they were telling me: no, no, watch how they breathe, how they walk, how their bones are structured.

But what did you learn in the bookshop, apart from what Borges taught you?

When I started, the owner told me: as you know nothing about bookshops, the first thing you must do is to find out what a bookshop contains and where those contents are located. That's something booksellers today have forgotten: they go to the computer. When one asks, "Do you have *Don Quixote*?"' they ask who the book is by and look for it on the computer, and if the computer says it is in stock, they ask the computer which shelf it is on. We didn't have a computer, we had to learn the cartography of the place. First, she gave me a featherduster to remove the dust... That was all I did for a year. And she told me, "When you see a book that interests you, take it and read it." She expected me to bring it back, but I often kept it... because you need to know what you are selling. Then she taught me that a bookseller must know the space, the inhabitants of that space, and how to talk about and recommend what it contains.

Which bookshops do you go to in Buenos Aires?

I go to bookshops—because I never buy books on Amazon—where I can have a conversation, where the bookseller, with a taste I may or may not share, talks about books. For example, my favourite bookshop here in Buenos Aires is called Guadalquivir, because the booksellers know what's there and have their personal passions and sometimes I respond to them and sometimes I don't, and sometimes I buy the books they recommend and sometimes I don't, but that's what it's all about—a site for readers' passions—and that's what I learned in Pigmalion.

Do any of the Buenos Aires bookshops from your adolescence survive today?

The bookshops I visited no longer exist. The Santa Fe bookshop, which I liked a lot, has become something much more commercial. The bookshops I was familiar with, like Atlántida, no longer exist, but there are many excellent new bookshops. Eterna Cadencia is an extremely good one. Then there are all the second-hand bookshops on Avenida Corrientes, and above all the Ávila bookshop, opposite my old school, the Colegio Nacional de Buenos Aires, and there's also a bookshop I've just discovered in a horrible, underground space, on Florida by Córdoba, that's called Memorias del Subsuelo—Memories from Underground—an extraordinary place for second-hand books, where you can find all sorts.

You have also lived in Paris, Milan, Tahiti, England, Toronto, Calgary, and New York. What were your bookshops in those places?

The world's great bookshops are small bookshops. In each country, in each city, I have my favourite shops where I always return. In Madrid, the Antonio Machado, but I also really like the second-hand bookshops, one on Calle del Prado and another near Plaza de la Ópera. What matters always is that relationship with the bookseller. And there is an important distinction between bookshops for new books and those for second-hand books. I prefer the second-hand ones, I like books that have a biography, I like to discover old friends and find works connected to the books I already know. Obviously, you always find astonishing things in new books, particularly in the area of the essay, the literary essay that has come into prominence recently, and I adore those unexpected essays on the history of hair, or books on public transport, unexpected stuff like that. It's true that bookshops have disappeared from many places. New York, which was a city of bookshops, has endured a genuine extinction, although a few survive as relics of bygone times. This has an impact on a city's intellectual life, on conversations, and changes the way one thinks. In Madrid, Buenos Aires, or Paris, you see people holding books. In New York, people are always holding their iPhone and I find that disturbing. Not that I think that virtual reading is evil, but it is quite different. The equivalent of that intellectual desert in the world of transport would be Los Angeles, where one never walks, and goes everywhere by car: a city where one never walks is a city of ghosts.

You have lived in several cities and continents, you write regularly, as far as I know, in Spanish, English, and French, and read in Portuguese, German, and Italian. You are, then, an "extra-territorial" writer, in terms of George Steiner's famous epithet... Do you feel you belong to a tradition of travelling writers?

I don't think of myself as a travelling writer, but as a traveller who writes, a traveller by necessity, because I really don't want to change places, but I'm always fated to leave one place where I am happy to seek out another. If I had to find a genealogy for activities, it would be that of readers who have resigned themselves to write. All my books come from my reading. As Borges said, let others praise the books they have written, he praised the books he had read. That is a statement which defines me. If I were told I can't write any more I would be much less upset than if I were told I couldn't read any more. If I couldn't read any more, I would feel I was dead.

So why did you take on the responsibility of managing the National Library, which prevents you from being able to continue writing and reading? Why did you make that sacrifice?

I think we have certain obligations and that each one of us knows what they are. I owe my vocation to the National School in Buenos Aires. I had one year at university, after six in high school, but they were so excellent I decided not to continue. They gave me the foundations for what I did afterwards. I read because of what I learned at that school, I write because of what I learned there. I have very few ideas that come from after my period at school. So I feel I owe a huge intellectual debt to the National School in Buenos Aires, where I was fortunate to have teachers like Enrique Pezzoni or Corina Corchon and many others, a debt to the city of Buenos Aires, and then there was the rather absurd coincidence that I met Borges when he was working as director of the National Library, when it was located in Calle México. The fact that I should come to fill, just over half a century later—and I say this both brazenly and shamefacedly—the position held by Borges, seemed like the inevitable twist in the plot of a bad novel in which the reader doesn't believe such coincidences were possible.

Moreover, you had never worked as a librarian...

Indeed, that would be the third twist. I have lived my entire life among books, I have thought about books, I have meditated upon libraries and bookshops and the act of reading, but I have never been a librarian, and I thought I was being given an opportunity to go into the kitchen after writing hundreds of recipes, that I was finally getting to sink my hands into the dough. I very quickly realized that I wasn't, that I wasn't going to be a librarian, that one cannot learn how to be a librarian without studying for a degree in librarianship, but that I could help those who were engaged in that task. At thirty I'd have had more than enough energy for such a task. I've just reached seventy, and physically I feel I don't have the energy to carry on for much longer, because this is a job that requires a mental and physical presence from early to late. I am in the library from 6:30 a.m., and what with official dinners and all the rest, I don't go to bed until midnight. Seven days a week, with all the travelling and constant problems; I mean, a library isn't a place where you only do one thing. Every quarter of an hour I have to solve a problem, related to electrical fittings, the purchase of books, customs red tape, trade-union issues, personal problems, there are 850 employees, a sick child, a divorce, the design of an exhibition, administrative matters, lectures, workshops, digitalization, in short... Every quarter of an hour there's a different problem, and although I have a wonderful team, it is exhausting. Although I'd like to end my days in the library, to be found one afternoon, on the floor in this office, I think I shall continue in this position as long as I have the energy to do what I have to do properly.

One part of your biography that intrigued me was the period you spent as director of the Library. The other that intrigues me a lot are the years you spent in Tahiti. What was your life like there?

As you know, our sense of geographical spaces is always imaginary. Places exist as places we have been told about, physical reality acts to dissuade us that a place was as we were told. I was working in a bookshop in Paris that a publisher had opened. I was twenty-four, twenty-five, and had just married. Then, as a result of a problem I couldn't resolve with that publisher, I decided to leave the job, before I'd found another. On almost my last day in that bookshop someone came to buy books who lived and worked in Tahiti, for a French publishing house, and with the barefaced cheek one only has when young, I asked him "You wouldn't by any chance want an editor in Tahiti?" and he replied, "Well, it just so happens that I do, we should talk." Then we went for a coffee and by the time we'd emptied our cups he had offered me a job at the other end of the world. I went home and told my wife we should look for Tahiti on a map, because we were going there in a couple of weeks, and we packed our cases. The places we visit as tourists and those same places when we live there, are very different. Tahiti is very beautiful, especially the islands that surround the main island, Morea; but, for example, if one lives in the capital, works in the capital, you discover that things are very expensive, because everything is imported, and, what's more, if you are working all day, you don't have the time to go to the beach (and I'm not interested in sport, I didn't go diving or such like). The climate is tropically humid, everything sticks to your skin, insects bite, books get covered in damp...

So... we can rule out any possibility of adventures?

I had no adventures in Tahiti. I worked in an office of Éditions du Pacifique as I might have been working in an office of... I don't know... Anywhere in the world, with the added difficulty that we lived there before the electronic age, so we had to make books written in France, edited in France, and then printed in Japan, where it was cheaper to print, in an onerous, drawn-out process. You had to write lots of letters. We had telex, but we mainly worked with snail mail. It was rather routine work that I did for five years: first we spent two years there, then I returned to France for a year, and then we returned to Tahiti with two daughters who were practically brought up on the beach. When that period came to an end, in 1982, the publisher moved to San Francisco and I had the opportunity to choose between San Francisco, going to Japan—where they'd offered me a post, because they knew me—or to try to start a new career, a new life in Canada. My book *The Dictionary of Imaginary Places* had been very successful in Canada, as had been the anthology I put together on fantastic literature, the house was Lester & Orpen Dennys and the publisher, Louise Dennys, asked me if I would like to live there. And I thought, well, if I want to have a career as a writer perhaps it would be a good idea to establish ourselves in a country that wasn't at the other end of the world and surrounded by sea. And so we went to Canada. That was when an adventure began. My wife was pregnant with our third child, when we travelled via Argentina, where my sister had married a few weeks before the Falklands War. My ex-wife is English and our daughters had been born in England. They took my Argentine passport away. They couldn't leave, I couldn't leave, and we had to travel to Uruguay clandestinely and from there we flew to England. However, they wouldn't let me enter the country where my son was about to be born, because I was an enemy. Finally, after a long time, I was given a compassionate visa, as they called it, and I arrived just in time for my son's birth. And we went from there to Canada.

In your last book, Packing My Library, *you talk about the process of saying goodbye to your library of 40,000 books and your house in France, a library that's now in boxes, in storage. Did you record it photographically? Do you dream of it? Do you know what will happen to it in the future?*

Well, there are photos friends took of the library when it was being packed. Yes, I dream about it, all the time, constantly. It has replaced all the other paradises in my dreams and I always return to that library, that garden, and my dog. The definition of paradise relates to the places one loses and my dreams show that, in my case, that place was my paradise. I had never had and will never have a house that is so peaceful, with so much space to think in and with all my books together, that are now in storage in Montreal. I don't know if I'll ever be able to put them on shelves again, before I die. There are projects with institutions in the United States and Canada, that could perhaps give them a home, but nothing's agreed and I have little expectation it will happen before I die. I have defined it as a library of the history of reading, because that is at its heart.

Why did you have to leave that house, with its fabulous library?

For bureaucratic reasons. I'd rather not go into that... But I had to fight French bureaucracy for two or three years and then I said, no, I don't want to spend the rest of my life doing this. At some point in 2005 or 2006 I made some declarations in France against Sarkozy, simply saying that everything he was doing was heading in a dangerous direction, although it was being limited by the French democratic state. In Argentina, before the military dictatorship, we'd also thought that the extreme right-wing shift would be stopped by the country's democratic structure. And it didn't turn out that way. And then, I added, that one could never be sure a democratic institution would be robust enough to resist the onslaught of a right-wing movement. Apparently some local politician from Sarkozy's party, in the town where I lived, felt highly offended by that and he persecuted me bureaucratically, which is the worst form of bureaucracy, trying to catch me out, and I had to employ lawyers, and it started to cost a fortune. At one point—you'll find this amusing, as a reader, but it was horrific—they asked me to justify the cost of every one of the 35,000 volumes in my library at that time, and the place of purchase, with documentary proof. I soon surrendered. I said no, we sold the house, our hearts were crushed, we packed the books, and here I am.

In Packing My Library *you say that you now better understand Don Quixote: when they destroyed his library, he lost interest in returning home...*

That's right, or rather, he felt that he carried his library within himself, and that's how he could exist in the world. I now "exist" in the world through my mental library. It's not the same, but it works.

In the book you mention some important sections of your personal library, like the one devoted to gay studies. Homosexuality and feminism, I've read, are two of the axes of the National Library in this new era. How does the section you have in your personal library regarding books on homosexuality relate to the later project in the public domain?

The personal and national library are quite different. In my personal library the main sections were organized by language, by the language in which the book had originally been written. Then, it contained everything, essay, fiction, poetry, and theatre. In the Spanish literary section there were even Russian translations of *Don Quixote*. Then there were special sections, like cookbooks, dictionaries, etymological books, books on the Don Juan tradition... Another section was gay and lesbian literature, a bit of erotic literature, and essays about the body. I am very interested in our obsession with labels: we cannot think outside the vocabulary of labels, even though we know that labels are reductive and distort what we want to know. It isn't the same to label Hemingway's story "The Killers" crime fiction, American classics, or men's literature. You know... I became interested in how gay or lesbian is defined via a label, and then my partner,

79

Craig Stephenson, and I put together a gay anthology we delib-
erately called *In Another Part of the Forest: An Anthology of Male Gay
Fiction* and that included stories about homosexual men written
by all kinds of writers, male and female. I'm interested in that
subject from a personal perspective. But the National Library is
something else. I want the National Library to represent all this
society's inhabitants. So we are going to open a centre of documentation of aboriginal peoples, of the original inhabitants,
in order to re-catalogue all the material we have. We are also
ordering and extending the gay, lesbian, and transsexual section,
expressly so there is documentation in the National Library for
those who want to find information on the subject.

In a small book published by Sexto Piso, Para cada tiempo hay un
libro *("There is a book for every moment"), you say: "From the
era of Gilgamesh, writers have always complained about the meanness
of readers and the greediness of publishers. Yet every writer finds in the
course of his career noteworthy readers and generous publishers." In your
case, who were those readers and those publishers?*

Fortunately, I've had many. My first generous reader was the
novelist Marta Lynch, who was the mother of a schoolmate of
mine at the National School. Her son took her some very bad
pieces I'd written, the first stories I wrote, at the age of fifteen,
and she sent me a letter, and she was a well-known novelist, a
beautiful letter I have kept, on blue notepaper, commenting on
my stories and encouraging me... It ended on this note: "I con-
gratulate you and pity you." I have also had many generous
publishers. I'd like to single out Valeria Ciompi, we're friends
now, she was my second publisher, but she became my main

publisher in Spanish, and helped me a lot. It is thanks to her that I have a presence in our language. Moreover, the Alianza Editorial books are so beautiful. You only have to see the wonders they did with the layout of the Spanish edition of *Packing My Library*.

I would say that your most ambitious books are A History of Reading *and* Curiosity, *both published in Spanish by Alianza. In both we find a style that is simultaneously precise and readable, slightly academic and very engaging. How did you forge that style? How did you come to what is generally called "a voice"?*

There was a collection of books that enchanted me when I was a child, "Classics for Children," with titles like *Treasure Island, Black Beauty*... And each volume carried an introduction by a woman, May Lamberton Becker, which always had the same title, "How this book was written." And I loved it because it provided all the necessary biographical and bibliographical information, but in a tone as if she were talking to a friend. I think that the conversation with the reader must be an intelligent conversation, a conversation in which one always imagines the reader is more intelligent, and one tries to say things as straightforwardly as possible. A Canadian, a publisher of mine, Barbara Moon, once gave me some marvellous advice, "When you are writing, imagine a small reader is perched on your shoulder, who can see what you are writing and asks you 'and why are you telling me this, I'm not your mama.'" It's very important not to confuse the first-person singular with the first singular person. I present myself as a character, like so many writers, so the reader trusts me. *The Divine Comedy* would be very different if Dante wasn't the main character. I am not the Alberto Manguel who inhabits my books, I select a few opinions, some of the ideas of Alberto Manguel, and put them in first person. Nobody is interested in what I'm thinking every minute of the day, what I eat or what I do.

The National Library was the venue for the final event in Dante 2018, a project led by the Argentine teacher Pablo Maurette, who resides in the United States, which has led thousands of people to read The Divine Comedy *in the first hundred days of this year...*

It was really wonderful. I didn't expect it to reverberate so widely. It was very interesting and moving to see so many people reading Dante thanks to social media.

Apart from teaching and writing books, you have devoted yourself professionally above all to journalism and publishing. What advice would you give young people who are thinking of following a similar path?

Borges told me that if I wanted to devote myself to literature, I shouldn't teach, be a journalist, or a publisher. But one has to live on something and we can't all write bestsellers.

That was strange advice from Borges, because he devoted his whole life to publishing and wrote for several magazines...

If you want to be an arts journalist, I would recommend you find a medium with a recognizable style—nowadays it could be a virtual publication—write an article in that style, send it in, and cross your fingers. But you must realize at the same time that you have to write hundreds of articles to make a living that way. The *Times Literary Supplement* pays some £50 for an article that may take weeks to write. *Babelia* in Spain, pays 300 euros. If, on the other hand, you want to go into publishing, my advice is to befriend a publisher.

As one clearly sees in Fantasies of the Library, *the MIT Press book edited by Anna-Sophie Springer and Etienne Turpin, the latest tendency in library theory is the defence of the collaborative dimension and the presence in libraries of curators and mediators. That is, libraries have been invaded or infected (fortunately so, in my opinion) by contemporary art. What do you think of those ideas? Does the National Library support them?*

It depends. One part of a public library's activities is the area of activities and exhibitions, and that's where curators and mediators play a role. But it's only the "visible" tip of the iceberg: the invisible part (which is much larger) is its technical activity: digitization, cataloguing, conservation etc.

In fact, it is a return to the ideas already partly formulated by Aby Warburg. In The Library at Night *he devotes a chapter to "The library as mind," where he says his library is ruled by a kind of "poetic composition." Is every individual library poetry or chaos and every public library prose or order?*

Every library has something of both.

When Borges was director, the librarian school was born. What is the most important thing a librarian must defend?

The very existence of the library. If a library exists, if a library works as it should, everything else will more or less flow.

You say in Packing My Library *that it is essential not to forget that a national library doesn't belong to the capital, but to the country. In Bogotá I spoke to Consuelo Gaitán, the director of the National Library of Colombia, about precisely that point: she is convinced that it is necessary to weave and strengthen the network that unites all the libraries in Colombia, whatever their size, in rural centres and cities. But there Medellín acts as a balance to the capital. Buenos Aires, on the other hand, has no rival. How is decentralization working?*

Provincial libraries also have their weight in our country. The one in Salta, for example, is outstanding. But we are working to strengthen them even more, to give them greater visibility and scope for activities.

Do you know if the project of creating a library in the Lighthouse at the End of the World on Tierra del Fuego is now a reality? What book must it absolutely have?

I hope it is created, I am very interested in that project, but I'm not sure it will happen. Of course, the book it must really have is the Jules Verne novel *The Lighthouse at the End of the World*. But a lot will depend on the identity they want to give that library, whether it is a library for everyone, a library for the inhabitants of the Falkland Islands, or a symbolic library enmeshed in Argentine-English politics... And the Library at the End of the World already exists, in Ushuaia, which is worth visiting, if only because of its name. It has a very good collection of travel writing.

Finally, forgive me if I ask you the same question you have been asked so often: was it exciting to be given the Formentor Prize knowing it had been previously awarded to Borges?

Every prize brings some joy and some embarrassment. Kafka said he had a recurrent nightmare, that he was in class and his teacher was praising him and someone kept coming in and saying, "He's an idiot!" "He's a liar!" I live in fear that some intelligent reader will say: "But that is absurd!" That reader could be me, when I saw myself usurping a prize that should have been given to forty thousand other writers I prefer. But at the same time one can't have the arrogance to turn it down. Borges said that modesty is the worst form of pride. So then, I am delighted, but I am hugely aware of the difference—it's almost a joke—of what begins with Borges and Beckett and finishes with Alberto Manguel. At least I was on the jury this year and we have put right last year's error with Mircea Cărtărescu, who I do really believe is as good as Borges and Beckett.

That Conundrum
We Call a Bookshop

On a flight between Guatemala City and San Francisco, I met a tough, taciturn trucker who told me: "We take only our travels to the grave." I agreed completely, as I was twenty-two and had endless leagues ahead of me. I would now add other clichés to our travels: our loves, our friends, and our reading matter. All of which converge in bookshops, spaces par excellence for what we have come to understand as modernity, a haven for nomads and foreigners, a land of book lovers, a cave or sanctuary where friends and accomplices meet, a hospital for flâneurs and beggars, a source of courtesy, and, in history and importance: unique.

Good bookshops are questions without answers. They are places that provoke you intellectually, encode riddles, surprise and offer challenges, hypnotize with that melody—or cacophony—which creates light and shadows, shelves, stairs, front-covers, doors opening, umbrellas closing, head movements indicating hello or goodbye, people on the move. Juan Bonilla recounts that when the Guatemalan writer Augusto Monterroso visited New York, a friend would drop him off at the Strand Bookstore at nine in the morning and pick him up at nine at night. Only an edgy, stimulating, and seemingly unanswerable question can keep one on the alert for eleven hours (allowing one hour for the Waldorf salad and cheesecake...) in the labyrinth that every bookshop is. A pleasing labyrinth where you can't get lost: that comes later, at home, when you immerse yourself in the books you have bought; lose yourself in new questions, knowing you will find answers.

The best non-fiction narrative I know about bookshops is *84, Charing Cross Road* by Helene Hanff; its great conundrum begins with the traits of booksellers. We've all read about the anatomies and poetics of writers, bibliomanes, and librarians, but what the hell does it mean to be a *bookseller?* The letters the American writer exchanges with the staff of the Marks & Co bookshop over twenty years, beginning at the end of the Second World War, dry up when her main correspondent, Frank Doel, dies. Only then does his widow write to Hanff: "I now also realize that he was an extremely modest person, because I have received letters from many people who praise him and from book professionals who say he was an authority." What does this mean? That modesty is a bookseller's main attribute? Is it true? In the best story I know about bookshops, Stefan Zweig's "Mendel the Bibliophile," the protagonist is defined less by his status as a secondary character in a Vienna full of intellectual stars as by his memory. This means, perhaps, that for two centuries booksellers were the personification of modesty; real-life versions of Funes the Memorious, from Borges's story of the same name. Ever since the business was computerized and (almost) everything became accessible with a click, however, memory has ceased to be important: modesty remains as the sole survivor.

"You have to remember that books must be the central focus," I was told the other day in Zaragoza by Julia and Pepe, who fell in love in a bookshop and founded Antígona twenty-five years ago: "That's why we strip them of their publicity wrappers." Theirs is a radical project: they don't have a webpage, they don't serve wine or coffee, they feed a community that, in a fundamentalist vein, prefers first editions. They are the penultimate Mendel, the penultimate booksellers to still carry their whole stocklist in their heads. In the second-hand bookshops on Mexico City's Calle de Donceles, where computerized catalogues have yet to arrive, it's a struggle to find anyone who knows anything: only after dealing with a legion of shop assistants do you come across a real bookseller. I'm not being apocalyptic: the history of the world is the history of a memory that fades generation after generation, of something that is lost so something *new* can be attained. And thousands of second-hand bookshops, in Mexico and the rest of the world, are still run by booksellers of all ages who love, know, and hold their books in their memories. But from the moment the modern bookshop first appeared, at the beginning of the nineteenth century, when windows opened them to the street, and the number of readers multiplied, as did the publications that were showcased, the most important development for the bookselling world has been the computerization of stock. And its extension online. Sharing one's own memories with the memories of everybody else.

In the end, a screen encompasses less than the gaze of someone who walks into a bookshop to browse. That's why a physical bookshop is superior to a virtual one: it's still possible—for the moment—for it to create better contexts. Complex systems. At a planetary level. A literary bookshop opens up lines for establishing relationships and fugues, brings thousands of titles, designs, and publishers' logos into conversation. It functions as a surrealist machine making unexpected analogies. Therein lies the challenge in the two dimensions of every book project: ensuring that books are the focus of those scant centimetres of pixellation and those solid, three-dimensional square metres, but also creating a place for other protagonists in the world of books, like writers, or the booksellers themselves. Bookshops should show off, on their walls and webpages, the writers who have visited them and the booksellers who have made them what they are. It's strange that this happens in cafés and restaurants of distinction but is so infrequent in bookshops. In *Errata*, George Steiner evokes the places that were as important to his education as schools, and bears witness to the legendary Gotham Book Mart on Forty-Seventh Street: "Its walls were papered with photographs, usually signed, of Joyce, T.S. Eliot, Frost, Auden and Faulkner and more recent powers." Galleries of contemporaries, visiting books, press cuttings, and biographies: bookshops and their booksellers should shed some of their modesty and make their histories more visible. Histories that are declarations of intention, and a genealogy.

Memory and modesty are poor allies. Only by being aware of the importance of book professionals in cultural history will we preserve their legacy. The genealogical tree of republican booksellers can still be pursued from Lima to Montevideo, from Buenos Aires to Havana, from Caracas to Seville. On both sides of the Atlantic, their traces are bridges shrouded in mist, and it is up to us to redefine their surroundings. Bridges like the one Eliseo Torres crossed due to the Spanish Civil War, or the one that led Abelardo Linares to buy from Torres's widow the million books the Galician left in his Manhattan bookshop. This was one of the book streams that fed the Renacimiento bookshop in

Seville, whose name (Renaissance, in English) couldn't be more inspiring. Like so many others before and after, Torres was a publisher *and* a bookseller; Renacimiento is also a publishing house. And Iberoamericana in Frankfurt and Madrid. And Laie and La Central in Barcelona. And Eterna Cadencia in Buenos Aires. And Maruzen in Tokyo. In fact, it is difficult to find great bookshops across the world that haven't also been involved in publishing books. I remember the volume published by Berlin's Autorenbuchhandlung to commemorate the shop's thirty-fifth anniversary. Hans Magnus Enzensberger, Jonathan Franzen, Péter Esterházy, Elfriede Jelinek, and many other well-known writers were brought together in an anthology of texts and images expressly created to pay homage to a bookshop that played a key role in the reunification of Germany, in democracy and capitalism. Because all bookshops are local and global; they are political nodes and businesses, embassies of democracy and free trade.

The conundrums a bookshop poses aren't interchangeable, but they are personal. Every reader has their own bookshops, their own collection, and their own memories. Before books nourished the library in Alexandria, before sellers on the hoof sold books at Europe's inns, before literary criticism and the novel and the printing-press were invented, before Diderot wrote, in his *Letter on the Book Trade*, that the "stocks of a bookseller are the base of his business and his fortune," before the Roca bookshop opened in Manresa (we're in 1824), or the Calatrava religious bookshop opened in Madrid (we're in 1873), before Adrianne Monnier and Sylvia Beach opened and shut their legendary bookshops on Rue de l'Odéon in Paris, before—even—George Orwell worked in Booklover's Corner in

London on the eve of the Spanish Civil War and that bookshop turned into a café for chess players and then a pizzeria, well before all that happened, I went into the Robafaves bookshop in Mataró. Because the others wouldn't exist without our first bookshops. And if as a youngster you didn't turn into a lover of bookshops, into a book junkie, it's unlikely you'd then decide to pursue them on your travels and research their histories and myths and—in a word—read them.

That flight in the Americas fifteen years ago was really a bridge between the Guatemalan bookshop El Pensativo and the California's City Lights. The previous Christmas I'd had a stop-over at Shakespeare and Company in Paris: George Whitman was still alive, but his body was increasingly ectoplasmic; he wandered around the corners of his kingdom like the ghost of King Lear. I bought books and postcards in the three book-shops: I asked for visiting cards and commemorative booklets; I took photos and notes. Over time, I discovered that Lawrence Ferlinghetti had created San Francisco's Beat bookshop by imi-tating Walt Whitman's model. And that on a chessboard in a corner of Lima's El Virrey, there were marks left by exiles driven out of Montevideo by Operation Condor (the US-led campaign to liquidate left-wing opposition in the southern cone of Latin America from 1975 onwards), and of the bookshops that the Sanseviero family had owned in other Latin American cities. And that Altaïr in Barcelona was inspired by Ulysse, the space created by the great traveller Catherine Domain. And that there were many bookshops that shared a name in the same lan-guage or in several: Odisea, Antígona, Central, Ciudad, Laberinto, Rayuela, Bartleby and Co. And that's how my own questions, my own hypotheses and networks began: my own collection of bookshops. I soon became aware that it was impossible to visit each one, because between one journey and the next, some have disappeared, or moved, or acquired a profile that asks another question. Everyone builds their own bridges—more or less foreshortened, more or less forgettable—often on columns sustained only by a whim. And by love. The discovery, the last time I was in Istanbul, of Pandora, which is divided between two currents: texts in Turkish and texts in English; my visit in Bogotá to the grandiose, white Fondo de Cultura Económica bookshop; the time spent among the wood of The Book Lounge and The Hill of Content during my days in Cape Town and Melbourne—all were less emotional than my return to the bookshops I already knew. To Clásica y Moderna in Buenos Aires, to Stanfords in London, to Bertrand in Lisbon. Next year I will go back to Green Apple Books in San Francisco, which is less famous but just as memorable as City Lights. Persisting. Rewriting. Always failing, but each time getting a bit better. Witnessing whether they've frozen or changed. Mystifying in order to demystify—since that's what all this is about. Building layers of reading. Adding a few lines to the book of sand in a history that has yet to be written. José Saramago said that being a bookseller is like being in love for life. In that sense, being a reader and a traveller is like being a bookseller. And I know this may sound clichéd and facile, but the fact is, there is already enough pessimism in the world as it is.

Fictional Libraries

I   THE COMMON HERITAGE

In tenth-century Persia the Great Visir al-Sahib ibn Abbad al-Qasim "transported his collection of 17,000 volumes by means of a caravan of four hundred camels trained to ride in alphabetical order, so they would never be separated," as Alberto Manguel tells us in *A History of Reading*.

From the library in Alexandria to the present day, human beings have never ceased to imagine, build, populate, destroy, save, burn, refurbish, rebuild, and even defend their libraries tooth and nail. Animals who collect, hoarding addicts, another name for *homo sapiens sapiens* could have been *homo librarium*, because ordering according to alphabet, genre, or passion is already part of our DNA—those terabytes of micro-filmed information; that miniature, biological, portable library everyone carries in their veins and flesh—because the need to order our memories is genetic.

Literature, architecture, painting, film, comics, and television have all recognized this human need, whose rush is matched only by desire, to accumulate and classify books. Because it belongs to the constellation of what excites and terrifies that we

95

have created from images, stories, and myths; imagination transformed into matter, where the librarians of ancient Alexandria coexist with the timeless librarians of Borges's Library of Babel; readers delve into anarchic Sherlock Holmes alongside methodical Bouvard and Pécuchet; minimalist libraries like David Copperfield's paternal inheritance, kept on the top floor of his house; and the inter-stellar kind we find in Isaac Asimov's novels, or in sci-fi films.

Young Copperfield read as if his life depended on it, feeding—with *Don Quixote*, *Robinson Crusoe*, or *Tom Jones*—the hope that a better life existed, identifying with the heroes and anti-heroes in his reading and wanting to be like them. Reading as desire and escape is ever present from the late Middle Ages. We know, from at least Paolo and Francesca onwards, that reading about love produces monsters. Modern readers, like Madame Bovary or La Regenta, suffer precisely because the books they consume don't provide models that help them to be happy; that is, to come to terms with reality. Long before those two women's imaginary grandfather, Alonso Quijano, was transformed into his own Mr Hyde, Don Quijote de la Mancha. His library was to blame. Apparently the *Necronomicon*, a horrendous book that drives you crazy or kills you if you read it, exists in Lovecraft's fictional University of Miskatonic; the book's possible existence reminding us that nightmares are made of the same stuff as dreams.

The Bible isn't a single book, it is a collection of papyrus and scrolls, of the canonical books of Judaism and Christianity, a hallowed library we now read in a single volume—an anthology of novels, poems, and stories. The same is true of other manifestations of the idea of the Book, like Diderot and d'Alembert's

Encyclopédie (comprising twenty-eight volumes in the eighteenth century) or Wikipedia (which, if printed, would comprise 8,000 700-page volumes), expressions of *The Book of Sand*, which nobody has read from cover to cover, that only exists in our consciousness as a selection, as myriad fragments. And that is exactly what reading is all about: storing pieces of a puzzle we can never complete in our memory and sub-conscious.

As readers we each amass our own library. We find solace and comfort in the knowledge that, beyond their walls, public, municipal, university, and national libraries are home to hundreds of thousands of books, a vast storehouse of printed knowledge. Beyond the walls of our skull, however, our own culture finds material form on the shelves in our study and house, to which we have been adding volumes throughout our lifetime, whether we have read them or not, that we will read one day or never open—who knows and who cares? What is really important is that we own and arrange them, know they are there, within reach, that we can touch, browse, or read them, partially or entirely, when we feel like it; have recourse to them, like Captain Nemo in his library on the *Nautilus*, or secretly at night, like the monks Umberto Eco imagines in their early medieval monastery, a labyrinth besieged by crime and censorship.

For millennia, every home possessed a small model of the Temple: a chapel, an altar, a corner consecrated to the spirits, the deceased, or the gods. Modernity has gradually erased them from domestic architecture, as the empire of the book and the proliferation of paperbacks simultaneously filled houses, turned bookcases into furniture as standard as tables and chairs, the surfaces of our daily bread. The library filled the divine, domestic space. The *Encyclopedia Britannica* replaced the Bible.

We all have our private, personal library, one that is also partly imagined. This essay is about the sum total of our libraries. About those fictional libraries that have been so read or scrutinized, so admired, feared, and enjoyed that they no longer belong to Count Dracula or the librarians of the Beast or Babel or Dr Who, or even to Bram Stoker, Walt Disney, Jorge Luis Borges, or Sydney Newman, but are now humanity's heritage, a collective imagination, the dream and property of each and every one of us, exemplars of *homo librarium*.

In other words, although libraries are fictional, they are real; although they were created by other people, they belong to us, because we are their readers.

II   THE LIBRARY OF ALONSO EL QUIJANO, EL BUENO

Don Quijote de la Mancha's library has no walls, shelves, bound volumes, or ceiling beyond a skull whose few wispy grey hairs are covered by a rather ridiculous helmet that he nevertheless wears with panache, conviction, and dignity—all the dignity Rocinante's ungainly gait will allow. Don Quijote de la Mancha's portable library is his head, which is sometimes mad, often sensible, and always appealing. When he speaks, he does so as if reading aloud from one of the many chivalric novels he has devoured, reread, and memorized, until his excessive reading of such novels and his lack of sleep drives him crazy, when he is but a skinny yeoman by the name of Alonso Quijano, *el Bueno*, and his books aren't yet constellations of neurons, bio-chemical miniatures inside his brain.

On the other hand, Alonso Quijano's library does have walls and shelves and just over a hundred volumes, the large ones handsomely bound, though Cervantes says nothing about the appearance of his small books. Paradoxically, we enter it not via the reader-hero, but through his censors: the people worried about his madness. While his housekeeper and niece—armed with holy water that could in fact be gasoline—opine that all books, without exception, are harmful and must be thrown onto the same bonfire, the graduate and barber decide to carry out an inspection, and view each suspicious item one by one. They eye them, leaf through them, comment on them, so we readers are lucky enough to witness an unexpected scene of literary criticism.

The first book they check is *Amadís de Gaula*: one reckons it deserves to be put to the flame because it was the first book of chivalry printed in Spain and is consequently the root of all evil; the other counters that it is the best of the genre and must therefore be spared. But the next volumes they review aren't equally lucky: several sequels are flung out of the window for being bad, presumptuous, and nonsensical. After so many are condemned, a second tome is finally saved, at which point morality and aesthetics start playing their strange game of tennis. Regrettably, the two inquisitors' peculiar morality wins out, their unhealthy distaste for popular, escapist literature, which they disguise with social and literary arguments. Fortunately, there are books of poems as well as chivalry. As a result, *La Galatea* by Miguel de Cervantes surfaces, the latter being a friend of the graduate and a man "better versed in misfortune than in verse." We then realize that the priest and the barber are keen readers and as fanatical about prose and verse as Alonso Quijano himself. Fans of the literary world, they were fortunate, or unfortunate, enough not to have lost their senses in books.

Or their fortunes. In *Breaking the Frame: Don Quixote's Entertaining Books*, Edwin Baker shows how unlikely it is that someone of Alonso Quijano's socio-economic status could have owned a library fit for a millionaire; one valued—in the currency of the time—at 4,000 *reales*, and also how unlikely it is that a cultured reader in the seventeenth century would have thought to bring those individual books together in that particular way. He compares the hero's library with the innkeeper's and that of Diego Miranda, the Knight in the Green Coat, and concludes that what makes Alonso Quijano's library modern is the predominance of poetry and fiction; what we nowadays think of as *literature*, rather than theology and the other disciplines that would have filled any *library* of the time; if, that is, someone were to make the strange decision to set aside space in their home for the accumulation and organization of books.

Cervantes's masterpiece is a classic thanks to its ability to adapt to a future it generates itself. Because *Don Quixote* is the novel that has spawned the most novels. Over decades and centuries, its library has increasingly begun to resemble the libraries of the new generations of readers who began to put theology and the lives of the saints aside in order to take up their opposite: fantasy, realism, the picaresque, romance, and horror.

Thanks to his doubly imaginary library, Alonso Quijano, *el Bueno*, would be transformed into Don Quijote de la Mancha. It is his brilliant excuse for leaving that village in La Mancha whose name nobody will ever remember, that place which could be any hamlet in La Mancha, every hamlet in Castile, every small village anchored in a barren wasteland like so many boats marooned in a desert created by an evaporated lagoon, so he can abandon his sedentary life for as long as the dream lasts, switch from reading—which entails the contemplation of other people's lives—to action, which means leading your own life so it can be contemplated by others, who are your readers; to expand the boundaries of his library and encounter dozens of narrators and readers, including readers of his apocryphal adventures, and become a traveller. Thanks to his infectious madness, Sancho Panza, or Sansón Carrasco, could also travel from the interior village to the port of Barcelona: from solid steppes to liquid sea.

The secret aim of that journey is to enable Don Quijote to acquaint himself with a print shop, to enter the ovule, matrix, and machine-room that nurtures his passion for reading, his losing of himself in books, and the womb that begets the books that nourish our libraries. And our travels. And our happy madness.

III   THE LIBRARY ON THE *NAUTILUS*

Jules Verne describes the library on the *Nautilus* in minute, fascinating detail. His tableau starts with a large number of books with a similar binding; he then broadens his focus to the furniture where they are lodged: copper-edged rosewood shelving—made from the coveted reddish-black timber of the guayacan—with alcoves beneath for comfortable, brown padded-leather settees; here and there are light, mobile desks where you can rest and consult a book for a moment, though it is the huge, central table that really invites you to study in depth. The library is lighted by four glass electric globes. Despite the luxurious furniture, the principal protagonists are the twelve thousand volumes that tirelessly roam the depths of the sea, the diffuse, murky, maternal waters of our collective unconscious.

Twenty Thousand Leagues Under the Sea is much more than a novel: it is one of those myths we all share. Jules Verne is much more than a writer: he is a popular axis equipped to generate compulsive reading, icons, utopias, and expectations. In the heart of that submarine are literary and scientific texts printed in every language, arranged with no regard to language, because Captain Nemo is a polyglot reader—from Homer and Xenophon to George Sand and Victor Hugo, from engineering and ballistics to hydrography and geology. Only two subjects are banned: economics and politics. As if the captain superstitiously believed that, by eliminating those disciplines, his boat could be spared the influence of international geopolitics.

For the first sixty pages of the novel, the narrator, on board an American ship, would have us believe we are hunting for a whale, the swiftest fugitive whale imaginable, that can furrow the seven seas so rapidly it seems to be teleported. Aronnax, the French scientist telling the story, is accompanied by Conseil, his servant, and the Canadian Ned Land, the king of harpooners, reminiscent of the tattooed Queequeg. Indeed, Jules Verne's novel can be read as an inversion of Herman Melville's: if in *Moby Dick* we experience the epic tale of how Captain Ahab's obsession with the White Monster becomes a fight to the death, with shades of biblical apocalypse, in *Twenty Thousand Leagues Under the Sea*, Captain Nemo's dark side, the overpowering desire for revenge that he shares with Ahab, never dims the light of his scientific, technological project, the progress he pits against religious atavism. Captain Nemo is a scientist, a devotee of technology, and a collector: reason can measure and understand everything, except his uncontrollable anger. Both books share an enthusiasm for encyclopaedic knowledge: the desire to contain everything humanity knew at the time about the sea. If real experience on board a whaler gave Melville first-hand knowledge of things cetacean, experience he rounded out by reading books that also surface in his fiction (the zoological digressions are almost as huge as the whales themselves), Verne, by contrast, nourished his imagination, as ever, by burrowing away in his library.

We shouldn't be surprised, then, if libraries are a constant in his work. In his novel *Paris in the Twentieth Century*, set in a 1960s completely dominated by technology, he evokes the future of the Imperial Library; in a hundred years it has increased from eight hundred thousand to two million volumes, while the librarians in its literature section, due to an absence of readers, are either bored or asleep. Conversely, the protagonist of *Voyage to the Centre of the Earth* visits the library in Reykjavik and finds that its shelves are bare because its eight thousand volumes are constantly travelling, from house to house, around Iceland; the islanders are compulsive readers and the national library a fragmented, portable archipelago. Ciro Smith, in *The Mysterious Island*, where there is no library, is described as "a living library, always available and always open at the necessary page." Nemo appears and dies in this novel: Smith meets him after walking through the *Nautilus* library, which is described as "a master-piece full of masterpieces." Sedentary or dynamic, monumental or nomadic, collective or individual, metropolitan or remote, the dozens of libraries Verne portrays are the backbone of his work, of his transmedia poetics.

After that initial description, the library on the *Nautilus* makes few appearances in the rest of the novel. Aronnax goes there mainly in search of explanations for the unknown phenomena or realities, like the island of Ceylon, that he discovers on his journey. Daily life on board the *Nautilus* is incredibly monotonous, with little in the way of adventure. In fact, apart from scenes like the battle against the giant squid or the crisis of the submarine getting caught in ice, this novel is more about knowledge than adventure. It is a hymn to positivism: observing, reading, taking notes, and developing theories on the basis of assembling thousands of specific cases, of direct experience of reality. "The spectacle of those waters rich in species through the glass panels of the sitting-room, the reading of the books in the library and the writing up of my notes occupied all my time and didn't leave me a minute to feel bored or tired," the narrator writes, and we can discern an order in his words: first, direct observation of nature; second, reading; and, finally, writing, thanks to which we can, through intermediaries, read and experience literature's mirages.

In addition to being an adventure novel and marine encyclopaedia, *Twenty Thousand Leagues Under the Sea* is a genuine library immersed in the abyss of our imagination, as well as in that of Verne himself. Politically, it stands out as being opposed to empires. Stands out reconditely, because a self-portrait is concealed within the portrayal of Captain Nemo: a self-portrait of the traveller and revolutionary the sedentary writer would have loved to have been.

IV   THE LIBRARY OF BABEL

Imagine reality without nature or gardens, without paths crossing forests or beaches. Imagine a world without cities: devoid of streets, avenues, vehicles, traffic lights, bottlenecks, skyscrapers with roof gardens, concerts, tabloid newspapers or sports news or advertising. A universe without planets or jungles or urban metropolises or squares or cafés or street-corners. Imagine humanity without dawns or sunsets, without kindergartens, orphanages, fashion shows, markets, or slaughter-houses; without families, family get-togethers and holidays, or naughty children. Imagine, in brief, a world of shelves, a beehive exclusively dominated by the tyrannical logic of books.

"The universe (which others call the Library) is composed of an indefinite, perhaps infinite, number of hexagonal galleries, with enormous ventilation shafts in the middle encircled by very low railings": thus begins "The Library of Babel," one of the most famous stories by writer and librarian Jorge Luis Borges, who imagines an infinite sphere without a centre. A bookish space illuminated by large globes of light, and a mirror beneath whose meagre, continuous light—due, I imagine, to the slow onset of blindness—human beings confront their state as librarians.

Librarians who, in this story, never stop moving. They are travellers. They are pilgrims. They are searching for a definitive answer that they will never find—because it doesn't exist: all responses are provisional, soothing injections the effects of which quickly dissolve in the blood circulating in our veins. Each wall in each hexagon has five shelves; each shelf carries thirty-two books in a uniform edition; each book has four hundred and ten pages; each page, forty lines; each line, eighty letters, as black as I imagine the eyes of the readers disturbing the beehive—wasps, pollen, and bees.

A miniature version of the universe itself, an exploration of the Pythagorean idea of a mathematics that rules over everything, the music of the spheres, based on combinations of the letters of the alphabet, the story finds a place for all those phenomena that have influenced the history of books: their burning, their worship, their messianism. There's also space for what didn't yet exist when Borges was writing, in the 1940s: the internet as a textual network of hyperlinks, proof that any sentence could have been written in a Sisyphean world that never ceases to exponentially multiply its information load.

Consequently, "The Library of Babel"'s twin story is "The Book of Sand," which Borges wrote thirty years later, and which tells the story of a Bible seller who offers the narrator a book with infinite pages. A book that is in itself an expanding library. A book that is the library of Babel. What the Book of Sand most resembles is a laptop connected to the internet. Like the library of Babel, the Book of Aleph and the Book of Sand are monstrous: Borges always talks about culture devouring, swallowing, digesting, and destroying us. His character is obsessed by the infinite book. He never leaves home. He shares his treasure with no one. He plays with the idea of burning it, but is afraid that the fire and smoke, like the book, will be never-ending. So he decides to hide it. "I recalled reading that the best place to hide a leaf is a forest," says the narrator. "Before retirement I worked for the National Library, which housed nine hundred thousand books; I knew that to the right of the lobby is a winding staircase that descends to the basement, where the maps and periodicals are stored." He takes advantage of the employees' lapse of concentration to hide the magical volume on one of the shelves eaten away by damp. It awaits us still in the catacombs of the National Library in Buenos Aires.

Perhaps two classic kinds of garden exist: the geometrically perfect French variety, with its sculpted hedges, polyhedric fountains, and carefully calculated perspectives, which communicates the idea that man can tame nature and control its minutest detail; and the romantic, ravishing English style, with its rustic meadows, would-be wild woods, which suggests a contrary notion: that natural beauty must be recreated in its exuberance and asymmetry, like a bonsai to a tree. Similarly, there are two main images for a library: one that is orderly and symmetrical, where everything is virtually attainable for readers, and another that is dusty and chaotic, a labyrinth that can hide monstrous books in its dark recesses. "The Library of Babel" is a synthesis of both of these. Order that can drive you mad. Infinite geometry that doesn't soothe, but makes us dizzy.

"I believe I have mentioned the suicides, more frequent every year," we read at the end of the story. When explaining his way of understanding theatre, Chekhov said that if a rifle were hanging on the wall in a work's first scene, a bullet would be fired in the last act. In Borges's version of that mechanism, it is the low rails at the start of the story that subtly invite one to jump (in a world where coffins don't exist, the dead are cast into the void and fall eternally, their only bier a rush of air, or mourning). Those rails give way to the reasoning behind the depression and distress in that Library, also known to us as the Universe, the history of which is nihilist and leads to extinction. Philosophy, Borges says ironically, can be read as a branch of fantasy literature. From that perspective, theology might be a subgenre of horror. Distantly inspired by the few lines the Bible devotes to the collective collapse of the Tower—supposedly leading to the birth of all our languages—"The Library of Babel" is a horror story: it simulates the creation of a paradise, but really speaks of the eternal existence of hell.

The Dogs of Capri

I   THE SELFIE HOUSE

Curzio Malaparte didn't bark at the moon, but at the dogs on this island. He recounts, in *Diary of a Foreigner in Paris*, that he learned to talk to dogs when he was banished in the thirties to Lipari, one of the Aeolian Islands, Sicily's younger sisters: "I didn't have anyone else to talk to." He would go up to the terrace of his gloomy house by the sea and spend long hours "barking at the dogs, who answered me, and the fishermen of Marina Corte called me the dog."

He continued to do that in Paris, in 1947, after fourteen years in Italian exile, where he was punished and imprisoned time and time again by Mussolini's regime, whose first steps he had supported as intensely as he would reject them later on. But he was answered only by the cats on the Rue Galilée: "I had to stop talking to the cats in the language of dogs, because the cats didn't like that, and insulted me."

But above all, it was here in Capri where the author of *Kaputt* barked and barked and went on barking, even though the islanders called him a madman and complained to the American soldiers, who asked him to stop doing it. But when Malaparte asked to see Admiral Morse, the officer in charge, he was told: "You have the right to bark, if you want to, because Italy is now a free country. Mussolini has gone. You may bark."

Is all this really true? I wonder as I disembark after the hour-long ferry journey from Naples. Compulsive liar and narcissist are two of the adjectives that tend to accompany the name Kurt Erich Suckert, born in Tuscany in 1898 of a German father and an Italian mother, who died exactly sixty years ago, whose pseudonym was an ironic riff on Napoleon's surname, and whose profoundly European life and work were contradictory and extraordinary: half chronicle and half novel, half incredible experiences and likely imaginings; a life narrated by himself in the key of what for the last forty years we have known as autofiction—a form he practised long before anyone else.

These crowds are very real; they give me a lacklustre welcome. A travel writer knows that a reader isn't interested in tourism. So I won't describe what's hitting the port at nine in the morning: the people queuing up to get on the ferries to Ischia, Sorrento, or Naples; the queue forming for the excursion to the Grotta Azzurra, or to get the cable car that, for two euros, takes you to the town of Capri or the convertible taxi that follows the same zigzagging route in the same amount of time, for twenty euros plus tip.

I'll switch paragraphs, and, via the art of ellipsis, I'm already on the path that will take me to a cinematic panorama, to a mythical house, when seen from afar. I've come in search of dogs and a gaze. The grandchildren of the dogs with which Malaparte conversed and the gaze that led me to his house. That house led me to a path. And that path, according to the map just given me by the Capri tourist office, links the house that was filmed with the one that never made it into the movies.

The gaze belongs to Godard: for *Contempt*, his 1963 film, he shot several scenes in the Villa Malaparte; but what caught my eye isn't there, but in the distance. Two men wearing hats are walking along a terraced path that's shaded by a compact arbour. The camera follows them down until suddenly it makes a movement no spectator could anticipate: it swerves to the right and shows the big red house, the stone submarine moored on top of a distant cliff.

And the two tiny figures on the terrace, which is also red and looks like a landing strip: one stays there, the other goes down the stairs. It was cinema meant to be seen in the cinema: whenever I pressed play on my computer, the silhouettes of the man and the woman gradually fused, chameleon-like, with their own pixels.

The house that was never filmed, on the other hand, is much less famous and much more discreet: Pablo Neruda stayed there in the winter months he spent on the island with Matilde Urrutia, in the early fifties. When the film *Il Postino* was shot almost half a century later, the island had become too touristy, had changed too much for it to resemble the island the Chilean poet had known. Michael Radford and his team filmed elsewhere, and the screenplay forgot to mention the word "Capri."

Journeys being what happens while you make other travel plans, the first thing I notice on the path that should take me to the two houses I've come to see is a third, unexpected house. A travel writer knows that travellers invented the digression. According to the blue letters on a white plaque, Marguerite

Yourcenar lived at number 4, Traversa Croce, in 1938. She wrote that every island is a microcosm, a universe in miniature.

Next door they've set up a shop selling typical products from Ukraine, Poland, Romania, Russia, Bulgaria, and Moldova. Capri has been a refuge for all manner of outsiders over the past centuries. The sophisticated lesbian friends, intellectuals, and artists, for example, who appear in the inter-war novel *Extraordinary Women* (1928) by Compton Mackenzie, who was one of their husbands (his wife, Faith, had an affair with the pianist Renata Borgatti). And opium smokers and addicts to everything, with Jacques d'Adelswärd-Fersen at their centre, were portrayed in Roger Peyrefitte's *The Exile of Capri* (1959).

Nationless and multilingual like Tangiers, both off-limits and safe haven, oasis and hell, Capri has always played with its advantage of being surrounded by blue. Societies spawn norms that aim, implacably, to catch out any deviant. But until that moment comes, all deviants, original minds, and free souls, all addicts and wayout eccentrics, try to make the most of the parentheses.

Yourcenar wrote her novel *Coup de Grâce* in 1938, but she spent the previous year with the American Grace Frick on a honeymoon crossing Italy from north to south, the details of which will be revealed in 2037, when it will finally be possible to read their correspondence (they never imagined we'd be ready for them several decades earlier). Marguerite Yourcenar, by the way, was the pseudonym of Marguerite de Crayencour. Literature, like journeying, is a bit of a *bal masqué*.

The travel writer knows he is a body walking under an ever more blistering sun, and as he has left his hat in his Naples hotel, he asks a couple of American tourists who are walking hand in hand along the same path for sunblock. Once I've smeared my skull, I leave Via Sopramonte and go down Via Matermania, which offers a lookout point at each bend. After turning onto Arco Naturales—a frame around a blue-white canvas—I pass through pine trees following a steep series of solid, cement steps on this island that, though built up, is nevertheless stunning.

At a certain point, despite not having a hat, I suddenly become one of the two hatted men walking down, my every step a still shot from a film, because it's only been fifty years, and films travel at the speed of light. *Voilà*, there is the antediluvian red submarine: the *Casa come me*.

Malaparte fell in love with Capri in 1936, at the age of thirty-eight, when he already had a literary oeuvre that included novels like *Sodoma e Gomorra* ("Sodom and Gomorrah," 1931), essays like *Intelligenza di Lenin* ("Lenin's Intelligence," 1930), or non-fiction works like *The Technique of Revolution* (1931), as well as his experience at the front as a journalist, diplomat, and conspirator. When he decided to erect a self-portrait in the form of a home, he bought the Cape Masullo promontory from a fisherman.

Capri's architectural norm was possibly set by writer, engineer, and mayor Edwin Cerio, organizer of the 1922 "Convegno sul Paesaggio" ("Conference on the Landscape"), which set the stylistic line (Mediterranean whiteness and simplicity) that still predominates on the island. But the house I have come to see is a monster or deviant or free soul; that selfie in a concave mirror, that red, straight-lined futurist manifesto, that *Casa come me*, because it is part of the bibliography of a great artist and appears in Godard's film. La Villa Malaparte, built between 1938 and 1942, was designed by architect Adalberto Libera, but is in reality almost entirely the progeny of its owner and master.

From that flat roof reached by a Homeric stairway, Malaparte looked out an infinite number of times, like a captain on his prow, and always saw the same legendary landscape, though with thousands of variants, because he didn't believe in history, and hence in pre-Christian and Christian worlds, the eruption of Vesuvius and the splendours of Pompeii, Virgil and Leopardi and Pliny the Elder, Andromeda in tears and chained to a rock, Perseus slaughtering a monster and his Malapartian sisters, the sirens, could all coexist on those crags, those islands, that coast.

Fascist and communist writers, American and Italian actresses, spies, consuls and military from the whole of Europe, and lovers were all on that improbable terrace. Only eight guests could fit around Malaparte's table; eight was also the maximum number that could stay there: the house was an island within the island. I'm now looking at it from the vantage point as Godard's camera.

It was mainly him and his dog on that terrace, alone with his dog, and as lonely as a dog. That's what we see in most of the photos that have been preserved: crossed arms, begloved hands aiming at the sky, astride a racing bike, preparing to pedal from New York to San Francisco in 1955; and with his various dogs, in his arms, on his legs, being stroked, ears down, in black and white. I press play in my head again and Brigitte Bardot is sunbathing there on that terrace, face down, nude, a book of black-and-white photos barely covering her buttocks.

And under that legendary roof, opposite the picture window in the lounge, over twenty years after he died, via the magic art of the play button, Malaparte repeats what he said in *The Skin*, but this time with the body and voice of Marcello Mastroianni, who plays him in the 1981 film adaptation: "He asked me if I'd bought the house as it was or if I myself had designed and built it. I replied—though it wasn't true—that I'd bought it as it was. And I flourished my hand and pointed to the wall of Matromania, the three colossal reefs under the cliffs, the Sorrento peninsula, the Siren Islands, the distant blue of the Amalfi coast and remote splendour of the coast of Paestum, and told him: 'I designed the landscape.'"

I'm happy simply to imitate Godard's tracking shot without a hat, and to continue to perch on this crag by the side of the road, because that's the most I can aspire to: according to people in Naples and various web pages I consulted, you cannot visit the house. That's why I've studied the scenes from *Contempt* and *The Skin* and the YouTube videos and photos that show those inaccessible interiors over and over again. The Abyssinian masks, Finnish carpets, paintings, and desk that are no longer there. The portrait by Campigli, the impressive fireplace, the great bas-relief by Pericle Fazzini, and above all, the natural landscapes framed by the windows, which are still there.

People who stayed in the house say Malaparte led a spartan life, with little attachment to the objects he collected there. He liked most to look at the sublime coast and sea, whether it was sunny or stormy. He also wrote and read and ate and fucked and watched television. It's as well to remember him like this at the end of the paragraph: hugging his dog, letting the waves sweep over him; waves that, at the peak of the storm, flooded the ground floor and spattered white, bubbly foam over the red roof, suddenly a muddy, matte submarine submerging, spying.

I've been here all alone for forty minutes taking photos (just one American couple walked by who asked me what that "weird house" was, and I told them and they reacted, *wow, very interesting, thank you, bye*) when suddenly two pixels appear, or perhaps three.

Yes: three pixels leave the house and go down the stone stairs to the landing-point. They could be a Hollywood couple: I can't see their faces, but they move glamorously, she with her white picture hat, he with his white panama, she in a white dress, he in black shorts and sky-blue shirt, she with a beach bag, he with a small suitcase on wheels. Someone accompanies them to the waiting launch carrying two suitcases that he hands over to the captain, fisherman, or taxi-driver. The couple board and say goodbye. The third person bids them farewell. And suddenly there is a dog at his feet, a little dog barking goodbye, that I can't hear, but can imagine.

The launch sets off, leaving only its frothy wake. The third person and little dog walk back up the steps.

Who can they be? Their steps cease to be stills and become what they always were: heartbeats. I walk off and the film-take and house stay behind.

I check my iPhone screen to confirm that I've taken a good selfie with his perfect selfie in the background. And I keep walking.

II UNDER THE VOLCANO

In *The Skin*, Curzio Malaparte invokes two geographical and symbolic totems: Capri and Vesuvius. Scenes are set in both places, which are constantly referred to. The narrator talks about the island and volcano, as he wanders through the city and along the coast, as if they were two corners of his own personal Bermuda triangle: the third is Naples.

A raw, sarcastic, distorted deconstruction of the American occupation of southern Italy, with the author himself acting as the unifying thread and translator between locals and allied troops, *The Skin* has to be the great Neapolitan novel. Naturally, Neapolitans didn't greet it as such. The author was persona non grata for a long time. Benedetto Croce publicly regretted having promoted *The Skin*, which was included in the Vatican's *Index of Forbidden Books*.

From Lipari Island—where he was under house arrest and learned to bark—you can see Vulcano Island: Malaparte's destiny was those volcanoes and islands. From my base at UNA Hotel Napoli, surrounded by a market that rises at dawn and disappears in the afternoon—hoarse, bawling stall owners, a pungent stink of fish—I could see both the Circumvesuviana Station and Vesuvius, dormant since 1944, when it had the last of its twenty lethal eruptions. At present, over three million people live within its threatening range.

In the first century—when it awoke for the first time, there wasn't even a word for volcano in Latin. The Romans simply thought of Vesuvius as a green mountain, which is why, when it began to give off smoke, Pliny the Elder tried to get near it to inspect the strange phenomenon; the rest is lava and silence. Those who died in the year 79, buried by pumice stone, gases, ash, and an earth in flames, never understood why they died. Reality doesn't exist if it's not preceded by language. And a journey is meaningless if one can't find the right words to describe it.

A travel writer must have a "fixer" in every port. Oppressed by the muggy heat, I called mine in Naples and he told me to leave all that and come here. A freshly shaven Raimondo greeted me, stooping slightly. He was wearing a sea-blue Lacoste polo sweater and the ironic look of a connoisseur, his hands in his pockets. He has never let me down, I don't know what I'll do when he finally decides to retire: he got what I wanted in just under twenty-four hours. He carefully took it out from under the counter, and, with the emotion of someone handling a valuable consignment, announced: "I had to fetch it from Sergio Attanasio's, it was the only way to get it."

In exchange, I gave him what he'd asked for, said goodbye with a "*Ci vediamo dopo*," and then went searching for traces of another traveller, Giacomo Leopardi, because that's what we chroniclers do: we're always following in the footsteps of others. Years before he started on a series of journeys that would end with his death in this city, he wrote his most future-laden poem, "The Infinite." A poem that speaks of the horizon as the frontier between two abysses. He was very young when he wrote it, he had yet to travel, but his entire life can be seen as an extended steeplechase, with obstacles every hundred yards and a different horizon after every jump.

I walked into Virgiliano Park. On my left, the lines of the Napoli Margellina Station vanished from my sight and entered the company of antique streetlights, the shade of cypresses, the smell of pinetrees, and warbling of birds, as I walked up a zigzagging path that leads to the lump of marble that recalls that the great romantic poet is buried there.

A security camera registered my presence. And a fire extinguisher next to the marble stone reminded me how absurd that whole commemoration was: the poet died in the middle of a cholera epidemic, his remains were lost forever in a common grave and his verse is all that is left of Leopardi's DNA.

But I carried on up, and was suddenly hit by a wave of cold air coming from an abandoned tunnel drilled through the hill. Its cathedral-like entrance was home to another extinguisher and a dozen pigeons—fluttering and cooing—who had nested in the hollows within that feat of Roman engineering, an astonishing tunnel that crosses the Posillipo hill, seven hundred metres long, five high, and four-and-a-half across, like the maw of a mythological wolf.

Tradition lies yet again: Virgil didn't commission the construction of this tunnel; it was the work of Lucius Cocceius Auctus, and it has endured over centuries thanks to various modernizations implemented by worthies like Alfonso V "The Magnanimous" or Joseph Bonaparte. Since the end of the nineteenth century, it's been waiting for a mayor to rival those predecessors. The pigeons cooed on one side and then the other, like lost souls. And the extinguisher reminded me that the powers that be like to go through the motions (it's been almost two millennia since the empire disintegrated).

Elsewhere in the hill, in a modest hollow of a few metres, is the grotto housing (according to that great liar, tradition) Virgil's tomb, back in the wave of heat. Temporarily shut by construction. Rusted scaffolding. Cobwebbed grating. Pigeon shit on the closure notice, perhaps from the same bird resting, corpse-like, in the darkness of that hostile, grandiose interior.

Three security cameras aimed—respectively—at the Virgilian crypt, the mouth of the tunnel, and the path I'd just climbed up. I wondered whether they and the screens might be connected, whether somebody was watching me writing notes on my pad that, with a bit of luck, might be transformed into this text.

I retraced my steps and, before leaving, went over to the guards' hut by the entrance: the television screen was lit and alternatively showed black-and-white close-ups of the monuments with nobody present: the lump of marble, the worn-out engineering, and the shat-upon grotto. A thin, uniformed functionary was watching an afternoon soap on the other screen. His plump colleague was checking Facebook on his cellphone.

Booksellers are *dealers*. They're also Virgilian. Without the local guides who show you what's not on Wikipedia, travel writing is meaningless. I went back to Dante & Descartes, my Ithacan bookshop in Naples—whose slogan is "Books Lost and Refound"—to pick up Raimondo and go eat cod. He'd found me another book I needed for my trip to Capri in search of two houses, two writers, two films, and one chronicle.

He gave it to me as a present, along with Erri De Luca's *Napòlide* (one of my writer-friend's books published by Di Maio himself). In De Luca's *The Day Before Happiness*, there is in fact a bookseller character, Don Raimondo. "He doesn't live here, does he?" I asked, and he replied, "he left some time ago, but he often comes back and stays at my place. Not long ago he gave a talk in Scampia, the neighbourhood that appears as a drug hell in the *Gomorrah* series, though it's actually full of cultural associations, especially those linked to music, and lots of youngsters who don't belong to the Camorra and don't ever aspire to."

Roberto Saviano launched his first book, *Gomorrah*, in Dante & Descartes, a reportage on the Camorra before it became a bestseller, film, play, and television series as well as his death sentence. He now lives in hiding in the United States. Giacomo Leopardi was persecuted by fanatical Catholics who contested his anti-dogmatic philosophy. Matilde Serao also had problems with her searing chronicle *Il ventre di Napoli* ("The Belly of Naples," 1884), and the polemic spawned by the publication of Anna Maria Ortese's *Neapolitan Chronicles* (1953) went on for decades. Although the city also inspires admiration, tenderness, and even complicity, it seems quite impossible to write about Naples without taking up a scalpel or drill.

"I occasionally exchange a few words with Roberto," Raimundo told me on our way to the restaurant. He then asked, "Do you mind if we take this side street for a moment?" Isn't that what journeys are? I thought as we left Via Mezzocannone and entered the alleyways of the town's historic centre.

"It's here on this corner," he continued a few minutes later, pointing to 22, Donnalbina, "that I opened my original bookshop in 1984, and it was an immediate, if modest, success." He said he'd tell me the reason for his good luck later, nervously using air quotes as he uttered the word "luck."

We walked a few hundred yards down the cobbled street, flanked by grandiose but crumbling facades—how the garbage stank under that sun!—until we stopped on the top part of the Pendino di Santa Barbara. It was a passageway with steps that one entered and exited under arches, its walls illustrating Naples's stratified history: from the Greco-Roman stones that were re-used by medieval masons and that go back to Parthenope—the Greek settlement named after a siren—to the small chapels lit by fluorescent lights and covered in graffiti.

"This is where Malaparte invents the most evocative, bizarre hyperrealist images that you find in *The Skin*, where a legion of prostitute dwarves offer their services on the steps of this passageway," my bookseller-guide told me. Hands on hips, with the expression of a bumptious elf, Raimondo recounted how the fiction was based on historical fact: that narrow passage, which had never seen a sunbeam, really had been home to a community of women who were dwarfish, due not to genetics, but to rickets and extreme poverty.

It wasn't hard to imagine—in the midday heat with that patina of dirt—those women whose poverty forced them to "reveal their dark sex among the rosy glow of naked flesh," while they shouted "Five dollars! Five dollars!" at the black soldiers, then closed their legs the moment the men disappeared. It is the least-shocking sequence in a novel where a father is paid to expose his virgin daughter's vagina and where a fish that might be a siren or a dead girl is served up at an aristocratic dinner.

Contemporary literature loves to recreate myths and origin-stories: in the beginning, Capri was home to the sirens and Parthenope's corpse reached the beaches of Naples after her quarrel with Ulysses. But in truth, mythology blurs or even forgets origins: Homer's sirens had the face of a woman but the body of a bird, not a fish. The Disney version merely expands on a tradition that began in the Middle Ages of transforming sirens into sex objects.

The real sirens were strident, horrendous monsters. Norman Douglas—the author of *South Wind* (1917)—was deported from Italy for pederasty (although he managed to return to Capri to commit suicide). And Malaparte, what can one say about his monstrous side?

"Here too there is a long tradition of dwarf books," Raimondo told me later, as we tucked into our plates of cod carpaccio. They were first printed in Naples when printing was born, thanks to a nomadic German publisher by the name of Mattia Moravio. "It has continued to this day," he explained, taking from his bag some of the mini-books he has published, and adding: "But the modern tradition began with the weekly publications from the Lillipuziana Library in 1892, the brain-child of Luigi Chiurazzi. He was the one who transformed the production of tiny format books into a distinctively Neapolitan product."

Don Raimondo is the living memory of the art of the book in Naples, this textual—and so often textualized—city. For years he has been threatening to collect, in an infinite volume, all the articles he has written on the publishers, printers, librarians, and booksellers of Naples. "When *Il Postino* was premiered, the centre of the city was immediately filled with pirate editions of Antonio Skármeta's novel," he told me before ordering a rhum baba. And continued; "But rather than being signed by him, they were signed by Massimo Troisi, the lead actor who had just died: I can't think of a better example of sophisticated Neapolitan picaresque."

I remember that afternoon and the following morning as a single, lengthy stroll, interrupted only by a café stop to search the books in my backpack for new information to investigate for real or to go into bookshops to hunt out some unknown text on sirens, Vesuvius, Leopardi, Malaparte, the dogs of Capri or Naples (my hotel was only a relative parenthesis, because I kept walking in my dreams). Although I walked alone, I never stopped mentally conversing with my guide, whose scratchy, vibrant voice is always associated in my memory with the city's voice, or at least with its soundtrack.

"I found no trace of Leopardi in his extravagant tomb," I told Raimondo the following day, when we were eating rice and beans in another restaurant near his bookshop. "Though I did find one in the house where he died, after climbing up one of the sloping streets in the Quartiere Montecalvario," I continued: "on Via Nuova Santa Maria Ogni Bene." I showed him the photo of the plaque on my cellphone: *Giacomo Leopardi stayed in the two rooms in this building between December 1833 and May 1835.*

And I told him it was an elegant entrance, with a large iron grille under a beautiful street lamp, but that the building was frightening, because ancient stone coexisted with cracked concrete additions, classical architecture with plastic guttering, washing hung out to dry, and a six- or seven-year-old girl who laughed every time her mother hit her with her clenched fist.

Hoping the southern air would cure him of his pulmonary edema, Leopardi lived in various apartments in Naples between October 1833 and June 1837. Piero Citati's biography describes his life during those years as spent in café conversations, second-hand bookshops, and the Neapolitan worship of coffee and the fruits of the sea: "it was a new pleasure he hadn't enjoyed in Bologna, Pisa, or Florence; walking and losing himself in the crowd, like anyone else, transformed into a body, a colour, a song, a sea-urchin."

Leopardi had a humpback. Children approached him wanting to touch it, half scared, half amused, hoping to knock off a piece of luck. "You've yet to tell me about why you were so lucky with your first bookshop," I told Raimondo. "That's true, let me invite you for an espresso and I'll tell you," he replied. By the bar counter he recalled an old man who'd spend several minutes every day looking in amazement at the window of the newly opened Dante & Descartes.

The young bookseller soon realized he wasn't looking at the books, but at something else, the walls perhaps, or the floor or ceiling, as if he were scouring the space now occupied by titles by Italo Calvino or Natalia Ginzburg or Benedetto Croce or Dante Alighieri. What on earth was he looking at all that time? One day he decided to invite him for a coffee, and the gentleman confessed that, in 1945, the building had housed a brothel: "He told me that many girls from Venice, Milan, or Sicily offered their charms in that place and... well, he remembered in particular a young woman from Bologna, who I imagine had made a strong impression on him."

Soldiers' blankets partitioned off the different "rooms." Raimondo asked him what he remembered of the nearby stairs from Santa Barbara to Il Pendino, and the old man said he remembered the women who offered their services leaning against the walls; these prostitutes weren't dwarves, though there was a ground floor with little women. Before he said goodbye, he said that everything the old man had told him had brought him "good luck," because in Naples people believe prostitutes bring luck.

We hugged and said our farewells in Gesú Nuovo square, where his son Giancarlo had opened a branch of Dante & Descartes. On the ferry to Capri the next morning, I started to read the book Raimondo had retrieved for me from their authors' homes: *Curzio Malaparte. "Casa como me," Punta del Massullo, tel. 160, Capri* ("Curzio Malaparte: 'Casa come me,' Massullo Point, tel. 160, Capri") by Sergio Attanasio. And *Neruda a Capri. Sogno di un'isola* ("Neruda in Capri: Dream of an Island") by Teresa Cirillo.

My eyes lurched from pages to waves and I thought that I too would be lucky and would write an account of that journey, that paradox, because a journey is always movement that writing interrupts, because travelling is always movement, and a chronicle also aspires to movement, but rarely succeeds.

III   THE SEA IN MINIATURE

Before Malaparte's dogs, goats were the island's emblematic animal: clowning, climbing mammals, perfect for those escarpments. Could the first sailors have mistaken distant goats for sirens? Couldn't their bleating have been strangely seductive, songs deliriously distorted by the wind?

In "Among the Ruins," his chronicle of Capri, the narcissistic British travel writer and fabulist Bruce Chatwin recalls that, "on the island of goats," "three narcissists" built houses on respective cliffs: Axel Munthe, Baron Jacques d'Adelswärd-Fersen, and Curzio Malaparte. As he revisits their landscapes in that brilliant chronicle (which can be read as a self-portrait in a concave mirror, given his interest in extraordinary, overflowing egos), Chatwin mentions Malaparte's book *Woman Like Me* (1940), "a series of autobiographical fantasies with titles like 'A woman like me' or 'A dog like me.'" There's no doubt that the selfie house was also a trans fantasy, but with a vocation as last testament or sarcophagus. It wasn't for nothing that he wrote about Mussolini: "Muss, a great beloved imbecile, a corpse like me."

I'm moving away from *Casa come me*, but the cliffs and pine trees are still at my side on the amphibious Via Tragara, which plunges, now and then, but never loses its urbane elegance, sweeping, as it does, past the most expensive private residences in this global destination for posh tourism. After leaving behind the ancient port of Tragara—a small beach with parasols and loungers—protected by those huge, eroded buttresses resembling ancient, comatose goddesses the map identifies as Faraglioni, I reach another of Capri's iconic buildings: the Punta Tragara Hotel. Since 1973, it has offered privileged views, which one can enjoy with a martini in one hand and an oyster in the other, from its terraces and swimming pools. Half a century earlier, however, it was a private villa that, in *The Skin*'s era, lodged generals Dwight Eisenhower and Mark Clark and Prime Minister Winston Churchill.

Three hundred metres further on, almost back in the town I left three hours ago, I stop by number 14 to spy on the ever-so-discreet Casetta di Arturo, where Pablo Neruda spent a few months. No plaque recalls this on the façade, so tourists don't visit, but a travel writer knows it is his duty to see what others don't, and when there's no response from the intercom, I climb up like a mountain goat and take a look.

I survey the steps that go down the side of the ravine and, in the shade of a huge holm oak, to the patio and house that Edwin Cerio, patriarch of the island's most powerful family, loaned to his new partner, poet Matilde Urrutia. That invitation was like manna from heaven. It was 1952, and, as a result of pressure from the Chilean dictatorship, the Italian interior minister had ordered Neruda to be expelled immediately. A group of intellectuals interceded, however, and the order was immediately revoked. Then: a telegram arrived with an invitation for Neruda to come to spend the winter and spring in Capri. Rather than go with his wife, Delia del Carril, though, Neruda took his lover; the person once called his *muse*. It is thanks to her that he wrote some memorable lines in *Grapes and the Wind* and *The Captain's Verses* ("then in your depths and my depths / we discovered we were blind / within a well that burned with our shadows");

thanks to her, too, that he published others that are cringewor-thy ("and the statue on the prow sails in the ocean of honey / naked, in the thrall of the throbbing male cyclone").

Neruda lived a humble life in Capri in a humble, unchar-acteristic house: a life of olives and wine and elemental odes. Although Malaparte and he were politically and artistically opposed, I realize now that the interior of Malaparte's house, as seen in the photos and sequences of *The Skin* and *Contempt*, are very similar to the interiors of Neruda's houses that also looked out onto the sea: the one in Valparaíso, and above all the one on Isla Negra. A travel chronicle tends to towards Aristotelian unity (of action, space, and time) so I won't begin a long digression on the trip that led me from Neruda's large house in Santiago de Chile to his three houses, to the three museums of this eccentric collector, to three types of poetic architecture. But I can perfectly imagine the three of them, for example, on Capri's Massullo Point.

I continued my stroll around Capri after spying on the house Neruda lived in adulterously: I read and wrote in a restaurant near Yourcenar's house; I visited the Ignazio Cerio Goat Centre (I remember the goat skeletons most of all); I returned to Naples and then returned home. And I continued to read Malaparte and about Malaparte, his dogs on Capri, and the dogs of Capri. And I watched films and surfed the net: one never knows when a chronicle begins or ends.

Malaparte writes in his *Diary of a Foreigner in Paris* that as a child he was weak, sickly, and driven by his imagination. The family home was on Via Magnolfi in Prato, the town where he was raised: "At the age of two, I removed a brick from my bed-room floor and when I saw there was sand beneath, I thought that sand was the sea. I spent hours with my ear stuck to that sand, listening to the sea, the voice of the sea." His father gave him a conch shell and he constructed his own sea in his childhood bedroom from his strange toys. He spent his time imagining islands and, when he paused to think, he saw himself as a volcano surrounded by deserts.

Contempt—cinema about cinema: a *mise en abîme*. On a secondary level, the film is about Fritz Lang—who plays himself—shooting an adaptation of Homer's *Odyssey* for Cinecittà studios on the island of Capri: amid shots of Greek statues, the tragedies of Penelope and Ulysses are embodied by the characters of Brigitte Bardot, alternately fair or dark depending on the scene, and her husband played by Michel Piccoli, a dramaturg commissioned to rewrite the screenplay, which doesn't meet the expectations of the arrogant American financing the film. In this fiction, Villa Malaparte is the mansion that welcomes all that arrogance. And in the fiction within the fiction, in the filming that takes place on the terrace, film and love are delivered in a holocaust to the ancient gods, the house's technicolour stairs leading to a large altar that extends into the blue horizon.

Alberto Moravia, who worked for Malaparte before the war on *La Stampa* with his wife Elsa Morante, divorced her when he was writing *Contempt*. When Godard was preparing the film adaptation of the novel, he suffered an emotional crisis that led him to divorce the actress Anna Karina, and an ideological crisis that made him a Maoist. These are the same years when Malaparte's last will and testament are filed—he died in 1957—and in which he left his house to the People's Republic of China, because, after fascism and before his death, he had somehow found the time to idealize Stalin and Mao Zedong, and to ask

Pope Pius XII to visit him in his bed during the one hundred and twenty days of his dying agony. While in hospital he received a message from the mayor of Capri: the island was making its peace with him, although he would have preferred his dogs to sign off on the farewell.

Several weeks after returning home, I finish *Malaparte: Vita e leggende* (*Malaparte: His Life and Legend*), the exhaustive biography by Maurizio Serra. He says in the epilogue that when he visited the villa in June 2010, he met a little dog, Luna, "still cowering because of the bad way she had been treated before she'd arrived, and she receives our caresses warily, preferring to sniff around a grassy area where Malaparte had created a cemetery for his dogs." He also mentions Alessia and Niccolò Rositani Suckert, who manage the house. I search for their email addresses on the web, their profiles on Facebook, but in vain. Who else does Serra mention? A pianist; a Finn; a Mexican woman. I look for her on Messenger. I find her. She is Professor Maya Segarra Lagunes. I contact her. She replies.

She prefers not to give an opinion on the house. I tell her I don't want opinions, but facts. Two days later she gives me her email address and says she and the owner of the house, Alessia Rositani, will answer my questions by email. They took a month to reply, but it was worth the wait.

"From the very first, I deeply respected and admired the house, but at the same time I was consistently intrigued and wanted to get to know it and understand its every detail and every solution they found," writes Segarra Lagunes. "The aim, in the future, is to keep probing its secrets in order to understand completely every one of the fascinating, original architectural solutions that even today surprise architects all over the world."

And then I do a lengthy interview with Alessia Rositani Suckert, who, together with her husband (the great-grandson of Malaparte, and son of Lucia Ronchi), administers the writer's legacy and estate, because I realize they're the ones who know that autobiographical house best. She tells me that Malaparte was aware that Italy and China had no legal relationship when he apparently left his house to Mao's government. "It was a gesture to encourage dialogue between the West and the East; he was always in favour of freedom of expression and opening out, the *Casa come me* also stands for that."

The couple define themselves as "a traditional family with Catholic values" and work with their son Tommaso to administer Malaparte's legacy. The villa is an essential part of that legacy: "it is very fragile and constantly mistreated by the sea, the salt, bad weather, and needs constant attention and that's why we count on a team of exceptional people who see to its upkeep, who are all daughters or granddaughters of Curzio's employees, like the son of his upholsterer." They have never received any money from the state for repair work: "We are young and can work to cover our costs, the state's money should go to hospitals and those in need."

Although it's a private residence, and they live in Florence, Alessia and Niccolò regularly lodge writers, translators, and architects there. Caretakers and the dogs are the only ones in permanent residence. I tell them how I walked around the villa on June 9, imitating a sequence from the Godard film. And that I saw people in the distance. And a small dog: "It was probably my son, or perhaps our Dutch translator, Jan Van der Haar, with Stephanie La Porte, who were working in the house. And the dog could be a black Great Dane, Agata, or our dear

Febo, a golden retriever, or Luna, our poor foundling, whom we often send off on an expedition to hunt the gulls that ruin our roof."

I ask if Malaparte and Neruda met on Capri: "I don't know, I'll have a look in the archive." I spend an hour and a half waiting and walking along the Via Tragara, via Google maps, looking for my digital ghost, flying over the *Casa come me*, looking for the change in perspective that will allow me to end this chronicle.

"I've checked from 1948 to 1955 and have only found this article, which seems intriguing," I read after reducing the island in 3D. Published in Chile's *La Nación* on September 25, 1953, the text provides an account of the day Malaparte visited Neruda in his house in Santiago. The author describes it in detail and concludes: "It is a magical climate: each item of furniture has the value of an idol or fetish."

Their conversation, in French, begins in the doorway, continues in the lounge and the library, and ends in the garden. The Italian writer is fascinated by the colony of conch shells that inhabit the library: "Nothing gives an idea of the sea like a conch shell, of the sea as architecture, as geography, as country," he writes, also relating how Neruda addresses each shell by name. One comes from Java, another from Mexico, this one from Ceylon, that one from Valparaíso: "From Capri, from Cuba, from the Atacama Desert: all the seas and all the world's oceans are in these conch shells."

That are miniature houses.

In Defence of Bookshops

"Every time a bar closes, a hundred songs are lost," began the famous "Blessed Bars" video campaign that Coca-Cola launched in Spain in 2014. The video appealed to the emotions binding us to those establishments and was designed to go viral. That year, for the first time since the beginning of the economic crisis in 2008, more bars opened than shut down. Why haven't Planeta, Grupo RBA, or Penguin Random House taken a similar initiative? Why hasn't the book industry set about defending book shops as emotional shrines for their readers? Amazon—which began to sell food in October—still doesn't publish sales figures. That's one of the reasons why, I imagine, there has never been a "Blessed Bookshops" campaign.

Other reasons can be found in Anita Elberse's *Blockbusters: Hit-making, Risk-taking, and the Big Business of Entertainment*, which uses statistical data to show how, in the internet era, it's still more profitable for big content producers to back just a few mainstream products rather than many niche ones. In other words, it makes more sense to invest a million euros in a single novel by Carlos Ruiz Zafón than on five hundred novels by other writers. The Harvard professor analyzes cases as different as Lady Gaga and Real Madrid, whose galactic model was inspired by Disney. She argues that, from a global market perspective, the fans who go to the Santiago Bernabéu stadium are essential as extras, because without them the content the club produces would lose most of its interest and profitability. I would argue that the same goes for most of the titles published by the big houses: they won't earn much money, but they ensure permanent visibility for their publishers in bookshops, online platforms, and the media. For Coca-Cola, each bottle or can has the same value. For the big publishers, there are two kinds of books: the extras, who are legion, and a select band of star players.

Of the forty-six products advertised on Amazon's main page, only six are books, though they are the first and the most visible. Paradoxically, at a time when bookshops don't inspire mass consumption, the world's most powerful virtual supermarket has appropriated books' prestige. Not only that: it has opened a physical bookshop in Seattle. This move immediately becomes global news and makes us forget the company also sells mixers, televisions, and frozen food, or that in 2012 Internet Bookshop Italia, which has been selling online for almost twenty years, became a chain of bookshops with branches across the country, some as spectacular as the one on the Via Nazionale in Rome. The mass media tirelessly broadcast Amazon's expansion while repeating that bookshops are on the way to extinction.

But old booksellers never die. And there are countless others who take up the baton. We must recognize and redeem these individuals, who have remained in the shadows while authors, publishers, and agents have become highly visible—even famous. Booksellers' memories preserve a heritage that can almost never be found on the walls of their bookshops, or on web pages. We are used to restaurants displaying photos of their most famous customers, so why don't emblematic bookshops do something similar? Casa Amèrica Catalunya and Xavi Ayén have just created two routes related to the Latin American Boom in Barcelona, whose points of interest include publishing houses, writers' homes, and their favourite restaurants and bookshops. We shouldn't scorn the non-material heritage that was once material and current. Or the economic importance of cultural tourism. There are many readers in the city who want to know where Bolaño bought his books, or where Cristina Peri Rossi, Enrique Vila-Matas, or Jorge Herralde still do.

Book chains are never going to be able to compete with Amazon. It's becoming clear in the United States that only independent bookshops, rooted as they are in neighbourhoods, can withstand its challenge. As emotive centres, as cultural centres, as centres for distributing books to those who still prefer to buy them in person. Most prefer to acquire children's books, hardback non-fiction, and art books physically. Gift-wrapping, dedications, and coffee are part of the rituals and artistry we continue to associate with book culture.

While those small writerly bookshops will survive, at the opposite extreme, Big Data and narratives of immersion will eventually converge. Our profiles as consumers are nourished by all the information we keep giving away, as, at the same time, the video-game industry and virtual reality fuse. Fed by information from all the books in our lives, fattened by our comments and likes on the internet, technology will construct a mirage of our ideal bookshop, along the shelves of which our literary avatar will stroll, spellbound. A personalized bookshop where every single title, which we can touch and browse thanks to virtual reality, will possess a virtue no real bookshop does: they will *all* be of interest to you. It isn't outrageous to think that this future will belong to Amazon, because, in the final accounting, it is best positioned economically and conceptually to achieve that end. But Borges already warned us that if you carry the memory of Shakespeare in your head, you will soon come to hate him. As soon as you have access to social media in your ideal bookshop, each user, in order to interact, must abandon their exclusive space and enter a common one: a bookshop shaped by terabytes rather than real books made of paper. And we will tire of this, too, and will need to seek alternatives with physical spaces, stable horizons, volume and three dimensions: everything our blessed bookshops already offer us.

Bookshops:
Second-hand Versus New

◠ A CONVERSATION
WITH LUIGI AMARA

Luigi Amara is a prolific Mexican poet and essayist. He is editor-in-chief of the magazine Paréntesis.

JC: I have no idea why over time I started to prefer bookshops that sell new books. The fact is I grew up in the suburbs of a small city, where there were no bookshops. Only kiosks, stationery stores, a tobacco store: I remember how I was fascinated by new popular-science and video-game magazines, and the new Marvel comics. At some point I began to go to the big bookshop in the city centre, and a second-hand bookshop, closer to home, in an area they called "the garden city." So the new books were on a shopping street in the centre (the bookshop, Robafaves, has since closed) that was on the way to the only public library in the city of Mataró in those years, whereas the second-hand bookshop, Rogés Llibres (which now only sells online, but is connected to the NGO that came to my place to collect the thousand books I had to get rid of when my son was born), was in a residential street, quite off the beaten track. I now see those two poles as if they were two scales of a balance.

I've no idea, as I said, why I was more attracted by Robafaves. Perhaps it was the new titles, the launches, or simply because it stocked the books that most interested me as an adolescent: role-playing books.

LA: Although almost any kind of bookshop fascinates me, I confess a real weak spot for the second-hand kind. There lies the thrill of imminent discovery you'll not encounter elsewhere. It's true that in an ordinary bookshop you don't always know what you're looking for and that there too you must explore its aisles hoping for that blind date you never agreed to, but you must nearly always do it swimming against a tide of self-help manuals, zigzagging between towering columns of bestsellers. As Virginia Woolf used to say, when we cross the threshold of a second-hand bookseller "a sense of adventure fills us": unlike the rows of more or less tame volumes on a library's shelves, or the ones highlighted by the marketing techniques of the big chains, used books are "wild and homeless." Even though they've been gathering dust for years in some corner, you could say they're still in transit, and that their place on a shelf is only a stopover on a much more random pilgrimage. That's perhaps what I most like about them, the quite electric possibility of an encounter, of a sudden surge: that at the end of a broken, whimsical line of owners and re-sales, of enthusiasm and scorn, the book that we didn't even know existed awaits, and suddenly ends up in our hands.

JC: I'm not sure whether the author of a history of wigs should use the expression "highlighted"... In a way, I think we've both developed the same idea: the genealogy of an object or place, wig or bookshop. A library would be to the bookshop, in the collective imagination, what natural hair is to fake or artificial hair. On the other hand, I don't know what bookshops you go into, but the ones I visit don't have piles of self-help manuals. There are so many current titles, recently published or from the last thirty years, that they too offer adventures and encounters (just as when you travel, an encounter is a source of fresh experience). I remember, for example, the moment when I saw on a shelf in La Central in the Raval a first edition of *Urban Voodoo* by Edgardo Cozarinsky, published by Anagrama with prologues by Susan Sontag and Guillermo Cabrera Infante. I had read the Argentinian edition (which I bought in the Athaneum in Rosario), I never imagined that the Spanish edition hadn't sold out...

LA: Perhaps the situation in Mexico is more extreme—hence my somewhat disenchanted tone—but I do think we are witnessing our once emblematic bookshops being transformed into book supermarkets, into large stores dominated by the profile of a book as commodity, and that clouds the horizon, where what matters is a quick sale and where self-help manuals and the most predictable coffee-table books have displaced some genres (including poetry and essays) to poky back corners. I remember, for example, how the Ghandi Bookshop used to be an unofficial school for booksellers in the south of Mexico City. You could converse and learn so much there! Not long ago I went there to find a copy of the Alianza edition of *Lives of the Eminent Philosophers* by Diogenes Laërtius, and the shop assistant not only had no a clue where the book might be, she also asked me what the author's surname was so she could look it up in their online catalogue... can you still call a place a "bookshop" where a computer has replaced knowledge? If today—and I'm referring to Mexico City—you want to find an old-style bookseller, one of those with a wealth of links and connections who knows how to locate a title in the broader picture, you have to cross the threshold of a second-hand bookshop: visit Enrique Fuentes in Librería Madero, Agustín Jiménez in La Torre de Lulio ("Lulio's Tower"), Max Rojas in El Burro Culto ("The Cultured Donkey"). Of course, ordinary bookshops can give you a sense of adventure, but I'm afraid they have banished their old sea-dogs.

JC: Conversely, elsewhere, megastores are on the retreat. Just think of the United States and the debacle that is Barnes & Noble, and the closure of Borders; or Spain, where I believe the economic crisis has boosted smaller establishments and put a question mark over big ones. On the other hand, I always felt at a loss on Calle Donceles in D.F.: there were no online computers or booksellers who knew what they were selling. I felt quite dizzy at the sight of all those books that might be of interest, buried by a huge, anonymous, drab, out-of-date mass. I prefer order and a computer to chaos, dust, and that feeling of impotence.

LA: Book supermarkets are growing here and collapsing over there, while neighbourhood bookshops prosper and fade at the speed of mushrooms; Amazon dominates the horizon like the unblinking eye of a cruel god, and second-hand shops are experiencing a fetishist euphoria in the midst of the digital era... It might seem foolish to point this out to the author of *Bookshops*, a book that is also an infectious journey, but in this motley, everchanging landscape, perhaps everything depends on what we want from them, on the expectations that lead us to visit a particular bookshop. (Obviously, when the parameter is simply "vast areas," I much prefer the chaotic, shapeless, out-of-date mass of Strand to the neutral, impersonal, philistine order of Fnac). Disorder and dust in a bookshop—and this from an allergy maniac—can only be justified by its rewards or, to be more modest, by the potential finds there. In "Poor Collectors," Walter Benjamin doesn't boast about his talents as a detective or his strokes of luck, as they couldn't easily serve as guidelines or useful advice for those infected by bibliomania. However, as I'm not driven by any didactic ambitions, I'll tell you now, I hope as modestly as possible, how I came to find my greatest bookish treasures. When vertigo was beginning to turn to impotence in a second-hand bookshop in the centre of Mexico City, a shabby, dismal, book-cum-sweetshop I had entered because the combination on offer was so unusual (because that's what it was, an offering and not, as it might seem at first sight, despair incarnate), and while I was buying for twenty pesos—because the shop assistant had made my day by theorizing about the complementarity of sugar and reading—"An Outpost of Progress" by Joseph Conrad, I saw them: two beige, rather aged volumes that were nevertheless in perfect condition and that were calling out, like Alice's little bottle of potion: "Drink me." Each one cost seventy pesos and I had less than a hundred and twenty in my pocket, but the bookseller agreed to let me take all three for that amount. Once I was home, I consulted the internet and confirmed the suspicion that was making my heart flutter: they were French first editions of Beckett's *Waiting for Godot* and *Endgame* (Les Éditions de Minuit, 1952 and 1957 respectively) treasures priced—the first in particular—in the thousands of dollars and God knows how they had ended up in that dubious book-cum-sweetshop in the centre of D.F. at a knockdown price... Had some unerring chain of chance led them to illuminate, half a century later, the unexpected boons to be found in the dust and disorder?

JC: It's well-nigh impossible that that could ever happen now. Until quite recently, hunters used to exhaust (that word again!) second-hand bookshops, seeking out valuable first editions. Now they've given up because booksellers always know what they have in stock, because almost everything is properly catalogued and priced online. Though some gaps do remain... And not only in the sweet-toothed bookshop you mentioned. I'm thinking of Havana, where people still sell off the family library without really knowing what they own. And not only in Havana, because everywhere there are families who haven't a clue about the goods that great-grandfather acquired. Last year I went to the Mercat dels Encants flea market in Barcelona, just before it was demolished and moved, and saw how at 6 a.m. half a dozen book-hunters were scouring the various lots of furniture and crockery to see whether they could find a jewel among the three or four hundred books for sale. I agree with you on one point: it's a world that is dying. That's probably why I'm more interested in the world of shops selling new books: that's where the future lies.

LA: A dying world also acts as a safe haven, as a reference point, and sometimes it's necessary to protect yourself from the thunderous avalanche of new titles—each one heralded as a "festival of language," as "the greatest must-read ever"—and seek out an older volume. In a way those dusty, worm-eaten books also hold the future. In fact, the division isn't so stark—in none-too-choosy second-hand bookshops you find piles of garish new titles that nobody should miss but that everybody did, in the same way you'll find the usual Chesterton and Lucians in the others; but those fragile, yellowing books, which have survived the shipwreck, also embody an idea of a book in their material reality and typographical style, which act as double protection against the rampant meanness in publishing today, like that counterpoint or sideways move that allows one to see the darkness of the present and head in other directions. What's more, if we move from books to a consideration of bookshops themselves, to the pleasure of visiting them as ritual spaces (you yourself practice and defend pilgrimages to those magnetic precincts imbued with culture and history), I believe one should defend second-hand bookshops not only for what they sell, but precisely as enclaves, as "erotic topographies" (now I'm quoting you), as hospitable zones in big cities that, like ancient cemeteries or archaeological ruins, allow us to find our place in the world in the long term.

JC: I often think that bookshops have been for me what churches represented for my mother at a particular moment in her life: both the safest haven for an anxious spirit and a place to visit as a tourist. In fact, sometimes when I've been on my travels, I have tired of churches and cathedrals, and even temples, but I've never tired of bookshops. They are places with an aura, though, of course, the aura is in your gaze. Relaxing places too, where order breathes tranquillity. Naturally, an endless place, in much the same way that libraries that house over a thousand volumes are. When I lived in Chicago, because of the snow and solitude, I spent lots of time in the university library and the Seminary Co-op Bookstore. Perhaps for the first time in my life I was radically systematic in both places. I mean that I came to consult, one by one, all the books in the travel and history of travel literature and tourism sections, all the books written by Saul Bellow or J M Coetzee, who taught at the university, or by Juan Goytisolo and W G Sebald, always accompanied by a huge secondary bibliography. That's to say, I read many and bought a few, and took notes not on dozens but on hundreds of them. Any library or bookshop has the potential to make an extreme demand on your time. You almost never choose that, but the option is always there. In a way, the strength of those places, their enormous power, depends on that possibility, that you could cover all the knowledge on a particular subject and explore something in such depth that you could make it almost your own.

LA: I share that idea of the bookshop as a haven, and as an excuse to spend outrageously long periods of time in them. Although I generally like to walk around them in silence—like churches or ruins—I have also enjoyed the most unexpected conversations with total strangers in second-hand bookshops, and that's made them even more enjoyable. I remember how, a long time ago, I started looking for books by Léon Bloy and J K Huysmans like a real treasure hunter; that was after I'd overheard someone who was looking for "anything" by Villiers de l'Isle-Adam, and who recommended them to me in the tone of someone who belongs to a sect; I'd probably have come to them anyway, pursuing the thread of associations that usually entwine books, but I'm not sure they would have meant so much. Something similar happened to me once in a new bookshop in Buenos Aires, where I sensed that people were snooping around, looking at others' book choices and debating in the aisles. Once, a woman, who noticed rather obviously that I was looking for traces of Witold Gombrowicz in the Argentina Bookshop, came over to offer guidance (no! to unleash a harangue!), and in the process invited me to a documentary on Gombrowicz that was going to be shown not far from the bookshop that same night, thanks to which my quest for the Polish writer opened up a new horizon I was totally ignorant of, and ushered into the bargain an unforgettable night.

jc: This conversation reminds me of how I started out as a reader. And it's a start very much linked to new books. My father bought them for me mainly in Pryca, now Carrefour, a big supermarket. I think that's where all my copies of *The Happy Hollisters* and *Alfred Hitchcock and the Three Investigators* came from. I remember that, while my parents went up and down the aisles collecting the week's groceries in our cart, my brother and I played in the plastic ball area (there was a massive cone full of balls: you had to collect them from the bottom of the cone and throw them four or five metres up into the top of the cone; it was a kind of huge hourglass whose grains of sand were brightly coloured balls printed with figures of Barça players or characters from *Dragon Ball*), or looking at books in the bookshop area (in a corner plastered with posters, mostly of cars, but also two or three of Sabrina or Pamela Anderson in the skimpiest of swimsuits). Later, when my father began to work as a representative for the Readers' Circle in his spare time, other new books started to come my way, by Agatha Christie for example. Now and then my father would come home with some of the old books he'd found, as he constantly moved around working for Telefónica in a nearby town, but I never fell in love with those books, I can't remember a single title; perhaps I was put off by the fact that they'd been read and enjoyed by other children, like second- or third-hand toys. Consequently, my humble origins (lower-middle class, as my parents said) were mostly connected to new books. If you think about it, shops that sell new books are perhaps more democratic than second-hand or antiquarian bookshops. For starters, there's a single price, you can't bargain, all customers are on an equal footing, (even those, like myself, whose parents didn't bring us up as book fanatics); while in second-hand shops, though most books are cheaper, not only can you haggle over the price, you also find bibliographical jewels, books that are worth much more. In the same vein, I've never liked a book of mine to be signed by someone else, dedicated to someone else, let alone annotated by someone else. This morning, when I was reading *Joseph Fouché: Portrait of a Politician*, by Stefan Zweig, I heard the sound my pencil made as it skimmed across the paper (I always read holding a pencil, usually from Ikea, for me a visit to Ikea is an excuse to steal pencils, which often double as bookmarks, for reading: years later, I sometimes take a book from a shelf and realize there's a pencil buried in its pages, which reminds me where I stopped reading), and I realized that this is one of the reasons I don't read on my iPad now, because there are reactions in your underlining, tactile movements, textures, a series of stimuli to your memory that don't exist in digital space (or at least that don't work for me: I read to remember and think, not to escape, I need those memories of my reads).

LA: In my case, all those "physical" aspects around the act of reading that make it "more real"—if that actually means anything—contribute to my fondness for second-hand bookshops. I have to confess that part of their attraction comes from the morbid delight I find in the fact that they *are* selling books that belonged to *other* people: the sense of expectation and perhaps of doubleness at owning a book that belonged to someone else, a book that, to judge by its battered binding and unkempt pages, was once loved and revisited by that person who, for fascinating reasons I'd love to discover, perhaps a sudden death, was forced to get rid of what he owned and never see it again. A second-hand book, not only the book that looks used, with yellowing pages, but the one that has effectively been read by another person, whether in sorrow or pleasure, is in reality two books: apart from the printed story, there is the involuntary story the reader added as he or she turned the pages: a private, intimate story it's possible to glimpse through traces the book preserves like a secret, coded text. The turned-over corner of a page, an over-the-top or frankly ridiculous dedication, pencilled underlinings, specks of blood or sweat or whatever, mosquitoes or other insects embalmed between pages, the almost always circular coffee or Coca-Cola stains, the book dividers, the torn-out pages, the cigarette ash, the paragraphs crossed out in rage—as if there was something serious to be censored—the comments in the margins... All that (which would be intolerable in a library book) acquires a suggestive quality, every trace is a critical nod, an elemental or biting comment; here and there you find evidence of boredom, grief, or bliss, which help us reconstruct the reading experience that preceded ours, and then to enjoy and sometimes doubly understand the book itself, just as when you're in a side box at the theatre, you're tempted to engage in the art of squinting; namely, keeping one eye simultaneously on the stage and the other on the audience's every reaction.

JC: I love the idea of the reader of second-hand books as interloper, as spy, as voyeur. But that's exactly what I don't like about used books: the fact they have another life which isn't mine. In a way, a book implies the fiction that you can find access to a world, to a life, to a gaze, without mediation, simply by opening it (a book opens like a door). Although an infinity of walls and frontiers exists between you (the reader) and the narrative (the writer), I am attracted by the idea that you have more or less direct access. If a book has already been fingered and underlined, that impedes my reading. On the other hand, I must confess that when I'm looking at second-hand books in a flea-market I like to look for books that are heavily underlined: books that have drawings in the margins, dedications, postcards, or photographs in their pages. I really like these books that are like chests, that are miniature museums. I'm also fascinated by the different kinds of annotation. How do you annotate, Luigi? I use a system that comes from my years as an amateur chess-player: I put a question mark in the margin to comment on what I've underlined if I don't agree with the author or the style seems clumsy, that is, a negative response, and an exclamation mark when I like or am excited by an idea, or when the style seems original or remarkable in some way. If there are three or four exclamation marks then the fragment must be astounding. It might be good to make an anthology of twenty years of reading based on such passages. I was once in the Sebald archive in Marbach and discovered, to my surprise, that he also put question marks and exclamation marks in the margins. I found it was also the case with Julio Cortázar's personal library in the Fundación March in Madrid. It must be more common than I thought, and not simply stem from annotations and comments on chess games.

LA: And do you use the checkmate sign for paragraphs that scintillate? I've simplified my method of underlining over the years, reducing it to a series of geometrical figures: rectangles for paragraphs that inspire new thoughts, triangles with the top pointing out for what's valuable and pointing inwards for what I consider to be questionable, circles for what I feel is crucial and the odd asterisk for something really cosmic, for sentences or paragraphs that are really out of this world. When I reread these paragraphs, I underline conventionally: a pencil line under the words. Like you, I'm fascinated by that critical paraphernalia in other people's books, a genuine seismograph of reading as an experience that can be earth-moving; everything that, in honour of Poe, could be summed up by the term "marginalia" (and which has transferred to the internet, whether in blogs, in fleeting comments or collective underlining, as happens on Kindle). Naturally, I like to dip into annotated books of authors I know, but also of writers who are totally unknown. I recall that Charles Lamb talks about this in an essay about books that are returned to him "enriched" by friends, by writers who leave traces of their readings. But this custom of making notes in books has its problematic side. At home we've sometimes had to buy two copies of the same title because I'd already underlined one and my wife wants to read the book, not the copy marked out by my responses...

JC: And what's your own personal library like? I experience a very contradictory relationship with mine. Although my emotional bonding with it is strong, it's true that I have only managed to exert control over it twice in my life: the two occasions when I moved house as an adult and discovered what books I owned and where they were located. I always feel tense and frustrated by my lack of control and inability to know what is really in my library. I imagine that all writers constantly think we shouldn't write so much, that we should read more (or vice versa). I also think I should invest more time in ordering and caring for my books. I envy the mechanics of a bookshop, where several booksellers constantly work to maintain an up-to-date catalogue of their stock. Mine, which is so influenced by my life and emotions, is much dustier and more disorderly than I would like. I want to ask you why our books originate in our purchases in bookshops. Do we need to reflect on the umbilical cords linking tens of thousands of bookshops to several million individual libraries? Do you value in your own library the disorder you like to find in second-hand bookshops?

LA: I will admit to a degree of chaos in my library, though I try to maintain order. I divide it by genres or disciplines (philosophy here, poetry there, etc.), and within those shelves I adopt an order based on chronology or nationality: French novels are all together, as are English essays starting with Bacon, Addison, and Steele. Like Georges Perec, I'd have liked to decide on a fixed number of books (let's say 666) and not buy a book until I had conscientiously dispensed with another. But over time I've become a bibliomaniac—one who has barely any money, but who, like all collectors, is incorrigible, and despite the fact that every now and then, for reasons of mental hygiene rather than space, we go on a book "diet" at home, a few months then go by and we soon lapse back into our vice, and start to stack two rows on a shelf or get more bookshelves made. Fortunately (or unfortunately), apartments in Mexico City are on the large side and allow this kind of uncontrolled accumulation. But your idea about the umbilical cord linking the purchase of a book to the individual library where it will come to rest is illuminating and suggestive: it is the function of the bookish cosmos that making another purchase takes on meaning, like accepting the presence of a new planet in the solar system; otherwise, as happens with some books you receive as gifts or buy in a rush, they run the risk of becoming mere shooting stars in the sky that is our library.

JC: I've been thinking about what we were saying about the element of surprise. It's strange that we lovers of literature, whether we like new or second-hand bookshops (or both, or better still, hybrids, because if the literary bookshop model in the twentieth and twenty-first centuries is the one shaped by Beach and Bonnier in Shakespeare and Company and La Maison des Amis des Livres, the legendary bookshops on the Rue de l'Odéon, the platonic idea of that space would entail the coexistence of the bookshop selling books and the lending library), we know we can consult online catalogues before we go to a bookshop to see whether they have a copy of what we want in stock, or can order one, but most people out there don't know that. Which means that for the majority of the population, who see a bookshop as an alien space that's not all that appealing, there is the possibility of surprise. But that has all changed for us. On the one hand, we have the classic kind of surprise that comes from meandering, from the thinking with our feet and eyes that is typical of what happens in a bookshop, where we might find something we didn't know existed (and that, consequently, we couldn't find online), once the pre-digital element of surprise is no longer part of the bargain, of the first edition at a knockdown price. Conversely, we have the new kind of surprise, the digital one, the one we get from a different way of thinking: Google, from our fingers (on the keyboard, on the mouse) and our gaze, which wanders or surfs across the surface of the screen. That's how we, too, find the unexpected. The ideal is then to go and look for it in person, instead of enduring the dystopia of Amazon drones coming in through our windows. I'm not sure, but I was wondering whether that complex thing known as an algorithm might not be the new form of predestination, of objective randomness. Whether the whole tradition of surrealism, reformulated by Cortázar—whether that erotic experience won't end up metamorphosing into Google Books or Iberlibro.com.

LA: I'd prefer to think that we are more fluid and unpredictable than a machine can anticipate, that our likes and interests are beyond the most sophisticated algorithm, but I must recognize that one new thing that has surprised me is book recommendations made by cybernetic engines... And despite my caveats, despite my resistance to becoming easy prey to customized publicity sent out on the internet, I have clicked on it time and again, and maintain a more animated epistolary relationship with Amazon or independent bookshops in other countries than with my siblings... In that sense we are extremely fortunate:

the opportunities to be surprised (and for book-loving to be nourished) have multiplied enormously. That's why I think of myself as a gratefully promiscuous reader rather than as a fundamentalist believer in second-hand shops, or an opponent of the great cyberspace monopolies: I read everything, from photocopies to coveted first editions, from blurry PDF files to airport novels. Amid that promiscuity or eclecticism, I single out, for all the reasons I've mentioned, second-hand books, those books where I can glimpse the shadow of someone else's hand, a tacit companion who got there and turned those pages before I did.

JC: As everything comes *afterwards* (not always *late*), it was while flying back from Rome today that I really grasped what I'd meant to say in our conversation about shops that sell new or second-hand books, etc. I found the answer in *Hope Against Hope*, the brutal memoirs of Nadezhda Mandelstam from 1938. They imprison her husband, Osip, and the first thing she does is pawn his books, the books he so loved, in a second-hand bookshop in order to to be able to send him money, provisions, his basic needs. In return, she receives a short message that's also very basic: the poet has died. Everything is there. In her gesture and in their reply (the bureaucracy, the Cheka, and Stalin). That's what second-hand bookshops are. They are death. They are readers who have disappeared, inheritances that have been wasted, poverty, emptied houses whose libraries have been sold by weight, or looted. What you find in second-hand bookshops, in one volume after another, are the sad, tragic, genocidal, dictatorial histories of the last two centuries. The dark side of bohemia is also linked to second-hand bookshops. The most lamentable form of the picaresque. You sell your books so you can eat. You buy second- or third-hand books because you can't buy them new. I know that's not always the case, but I think I've already said that I can't recall a single significant find, one really essential read, that came from a second-hand bookshop. Yesterday in Rome I was thinking how there are two kinds of antiquarian bookshop: the one selling books (and maps and etchings) that you can't afford to buy—luxurious, snobbish, collectors' items—and the one selling books I probably don't want to buy, pure bargain-basement, knock-down offerings, where you invest lots of time for an unlikely return. I believe that's why I opted for bookshops that sold new stock when I was very young, that are a midpoint between bibliophilic luxury and bargain-basement items. And that are consequently more democratic? Who can say whether I also opted for what was new as a commitment to the future, to a level of optimism and hope rather than for what was old, past, and surviving against all hope.

LA: Second-hand bookshops certainly have a whiff of death about them. They aren't mausolea, properly speaking, because things stir within them and change hands and even make people happy, but they aren't far removed, both in procedure and atmosphere, from the desecrating of graves: displaying and selling off the library (if not the mind) of someone who is no longer here involves a degree of sacrilege, and, in any case, the whole operation is shrouded in gloom. I discovered that in Mexico, and probably elsewhere, the figure of the book scavenger exists: a lugubrious fellow who wears black every day, whose work consists in reading the day's obituaries and confronting the family with the horrendous phrase: "I know these are difficult moments, when you are faced with many expenses…" I've often fantasized about interviewing him, but a sense of restraint or genuine horror has distanced me from that genuine scavenging vulture I could easily have contacted. But the fact is that death is ever-present in the books piled up in those bookshops, which, furthermore, are always gloomy; ruination and misfortune impregnate their pages and the transactions entered into there, which I think put into perspective the dreams of immortality that usually surround literary enterprises: there is something in the dust sticking to their spines, in the inscriptions from ink-wells now gone dry, that mocks the idea of posterity, and that, perhaps, is the source of their attraction as a counterpoint to hope, to the optimism embodied in new books, with their still dazzlingly white pages. The value of a first edition, of a signed copy, finally depends on the way they reduce one's distance from the author; although they are often seen as a fetishist mania, they are also a lethal counterweight to a deceptive abstraction, to a name that has become hallowed: those books are prized because they have survived, but, above all (I believe), because they reveal the undeniable presence of death where we usually expect to find life and intensity.

JC: I love this urban legend. The Book Vulture seems so plausible. I imagine him on the doorstep of the deceased's house, alongside the Art Vulture, the Crockery Vulture, the Antique Furniture Vulture. There must be a novel here in this network of men sentenced to wander daily through the obituary pages and the homes of the dead. A very Mexican novel, of course, given your very special relationship with death. In fact, the antique-books hunter is something of a scavenger in his status as collector. Hunting and strolling could be two different and

opposed ways to walk through the city and its bookshops. Tense
or relaxed. Concentrating on his prey, a rare, valuable book; or
open to the street, the marketplace, graffiti, magazines, new
books, and old stock. I'm fascinated by the relationship between
a journey through a city and abroad. I prepare my journey over
months and years, revisiting my own library and salvaging volumes that might be of interest (right now, with the prospect of a
visit to Rio de Janeiro in March, I found the *Letter on the Discovery
of Brazil* by Vaz de Caminha, in the Acantilado edition, which I'd
forgotten I owned) or else, above all, exploring bookshops. In
Barcelona we have Altaïr, which specializes in travel books that
are classified by country, not only maps and guides, but also
novels, stories, essays, and poetry. I never go on a journey without paying that shop a visit. And so books to read pile up on my
desk, the reads I'll pack in my suitcase. For example, *The Armies*,
by Evelio Rosero, waited there at least four months, until I went
to Bogotá. Yesterday I read that Mandelstam prepared for his
journey to Armenia in second-hand bookshops, where he found
old chronicles that interested him. I do the same in La Central,
in Laie and Altaïr. I'm more interested in wandering through
book markets when I travel than when I'm at home. Purely as a
browser, not hunting for anything in particular.

LA: It's true, there's a glint in the eye of a stroller when he's
hunting down a find. But equally in second-hand bookshops one
has ample opportunity to merely meander, with no thought of
the hunt, and that's what I like to do (although sometimes, when
I'm opposite a shelf, my eyes are a lynx's and my canines are
ready…). As for the book vulture, he's much more than an urban
legend, though he's certainly waiting to be turned into a novel.

As you can imagine, in this country they don't wait for death to come: the vulture, or, in this case, the falcon or bird of prey, is usually in cahoots with removal firms and, in the time it takes to reach the new house, he's inside the removal lorry, already having niftily purloined the ten or twenty most valuable books from the library in transit. Apparently, they always have the houses with valuable collections in their sights. My bookseller friends have invited me to a clandestine, early-morning book market where these spoils, the fruits of looting or scavenging, get "laundered." I really must go one of these days.

JC: The more I think about our absurdly polarized conversation, the more polarized I feel. I'm now wondering whether the second-hand bookshop, with its crypt mystique, isn't a link to the old god of the Book and Capitalism. Because if you look ironically at our dependency on cultural objects, our worship of particular novels, films, or records, it's obvious that it's as absurd as Sunday worship is to the eyes of an atheist. I'll be arriving in Mexico City at 5 a.m. one day in March. Let's meet in that clandestine market.

Bookshops Are Being Reinvented in Tokyo

"There used to be a famous bookshop on this premises, the Aoyama Book Centre, which had to close its doors, like so many others in Tokyo, because this business isn't profitable if you only sell books," states Akira Ito, the owner of Bunkitsu, who, like the rest of his employees, wears an elegant concierge's uniform.

"For us, going to a bookshop is a lot like going to a museum where you mostly look and stare and don't necessarily buy, so that's why we set an entry price of 1500 yen, which is what most Japanese museums charge," he continues with the fluency of someone who has had to repeat his rationale countless times since the project was initiated last December.

Bunkitsu became the first bookshop in the world to levy an entry charge from the day it opened, and, by extension, a global news item. It is the second bookshop to decide on such a tactic: Lello, in Porto, began to do so in 2015—146 years after it was founded—when it became unbearably touristy as a result of a misunderstanding: millions of people believe it has a connection to the Harry Potter universe.

But perhaps neither Bunkitsu nor Lello are exactly bookshops. The Portuguese shop is arguably a museum of itself;

with J K Rowling books in several languages and other brand merchandising being all they really sell—the entry charge is refunded if you buy something—it works like a museum shop.

At Bunkitsu, which is open from 9 a.m. to 11 p.m., the obligatory Japanese entry charge of more than $13 (US) includes all the tea or coffee a customer wants while on the premises. If you take into account that 1,500 yen buys you a coffee in an expensive establishment and two in any corner café in this district, Roppongi, you could say that Bunkitsu's charges a competitive rate for the stimulants it sells beyond its bookshop façade.

Or two beautiful, welcoming co-working spaces joined by tables and shelves full of an excellent selection of books: a long table lit by the classical green lamps you find in the New York Public Library or National Library of Argentina and an area of tables, chairs, and sofas next to the cafeteria.

However you look at it, Bunkitsu is a going concern. "We have a hundred customers a day and can pay ten bookish concierges," concludes Ito—who is being interpreted for me by Hispanist Kenji Katsumoto. Consultations with those ten uniformed booksellers is also included in the price, as is reading books that are on sale: most readers or customers make notes on their laptops about what they're reading in the expensive art, design, and architectural volumes.

Bunkitsu has generated a heated debate in Japan, because writers, journalists, teachers, and lovers of books in general have taken the bait, arguing over an inaccurate slogan that has nevertheless worked perfectly as a marketing tool: *The first bookshop in the world to charge for entry*. In fact, not only is it normal to pay a fee for a co-working space in Tokyo, you must also pay for your obligatory drink in a cafeteria. It's also true that the most activist literary bookshops—like Readin', Writin', Chekccori, Book & Beer, or Cien Años—charge at least 1,000 yen to attend their readings and book launches.

Three years ago, Tokyo's bookish side was heavily in the media thanks to another bookseller, Yoshiyuki Morioka, who was worried about his business's low profits. On a street at the edge of the renowned Ginza district, he created a project called "A single room with a single book" in the Morioka Shoten bookshop, in which he stocked just a single book per week: a novel; a book of poetry, photography, manga, art, or handicrafts; a fashion catalogue or even a self-published volume—accompanied, or not, by manuscripts, graphic work, or articles with a connection to the volume under focus.

It is far more difficult to sum up the concept of Bookshop Traveller, a café-bookshop established in August 2018, which, despite its undoubted originality, has failed to capture the interest of the press. Its curator is Masayuki Waki, the leading expert on Japanese bookshops, who defines himself as a "bookshop lover" on his web page.

Aiming to eliminate the problem of how to manage new titles and stock, he decided to transform his premises into a beehive. The store's shelves are divided into thirty spaces, with the smallest rented out for 3,000 yen and the biggest for 5,000. Their contents depend on the thirty independent—amateur or professional; booksellers and bookshops with their own premises, or with travelling salesmen or web sales—who decide not only which books they will carry but also how their shelving will be decorated or what objects they will incorporate.

One hundred percent of the profit goes to those renting the spaces. It's no coincidence that there are as many booksellers as there are days in a month, because each day one of them is on duty in Bookshop Traveller. Some hope to open their own bookshops one day, so here they can learn and try out their ideas; others had to close down their shops or are running shops in other cities and only come periodically to the capital; each project is a world—one or several biographies—on a spectrum that ranges from self-promotion to romantic dream. It's very likely the first metabookshop in history.

But it's impossible to know for sure, since millions of bookshops exist—and have existed—throughout the world. What we do know for sure is that China has 250,000 bookshops, only one of which, Mil Gotas in Beijing, exclusively sells books in Spanish. And that there are 315 bookshops in Barcelona, but only the recently opened Lata Peinada specializes in Latin American literature. And that in Mexico City there are 485 visible bookstores, and only two are secret: El Burro Culto ("The Cultured Donkey") and La Mula Sabia ("The Wise Mule"). It's all about standing out. About looking for new approaches, because their reliance on traditional formulas is one reason why bookshops continue to close every day.

Bunkitsu manages to be economically sustainable by questioning a traditional, hallowed truth: must bookshop browsing necessarily be free? Do HBO or Netflix allow you to view their series or films without paying your subscription in advance? Morioka Shoten is doing the same thing with the idea of variety; Bookshop Traveller, with unity. By levying an entry charge, zooming in on, or believing in, collective intelligence, these three innovative projects in Tokyo are adapting to a new era.

It's not only Japan's new independent bookshops that are adapting: Tsutaya is expanding by reinventing its extensive floor space. The company began in 1983 and committed itself for almost twenty years to online sales and lending—in parallel with Amazon or Netflix; but over the last ten years it has opened huge physical bookshops in several cities across the country, in partnership with Starbucks no less. The company also calls its booksellers "concierges" as part of an aspirational model that treats readers as if they were in a five-star hotel.

Tsutaya's most important shops might be those in the city's two most exclusive districts: Daikanyama and Ginza. In the latter, a traditionally wealthy district, in addition to thousands of fine art, photography, illustrated, and manga books, the store also sells expensive Taschen editions, antiquarian volumes, and works of art (like one of 2,300 copies of Jeff Koon's *Balloon Dog (Magenta)*, for 1,700,000 yen, or US$ 15,200).

The Tsutaya shop in the more nouveau riche area, designed by Klein Dytham architecture, is home to a multitude of magazines and books placed in sections where they're in dialogue with other, very select objects. The stationery section is extremely stylish, with offerings like Midori or Apica notebooks, Faber Castell pencil cases, or Montblanc pens, not to mention the wrappers that Tokyians use to camouflage their paperbacks while riding the metro.

Cooking being akin to reading, books on gastronomy share shelves with utensils, china crockery, and bottles of wine. The bookshops synchronize with the seasons: as it is plum season, pots of jam and jam-making manuals are on offer. Volumes about the world of cars co-exist with a racing car; those on history and natural sciences with the fossilized head of a mammoth.

Sumiyo Motonaga, the public relations spokesman for Tsutaya's headquarters, comments—via translator Akifumi

Uchida—that "it's all about creating real, physical, attractive spaces, where an individual can spend lots of time without their pleasure declining to an exclusively human level." To remind us that the internet's abstract, gigantic reality isn't natural, the building's architecture plays at alternating large and much smaller spaces, where consulting or reading can become an intimate, private experience.

Great, diverse spaces can also be found at Lisbon's Ler Devagar, Seoul's Book Park, or the refurbished Callao branch of Madrid's La Central. But perhaps the ultimate expression of this new tendency is Page One, a bookstore in Beijing's historic centre that's open twenty-four hours a day, where each major section has been designed with a distinct identity, to the point where you can visit at least six bookshops without leaving one.

If audiovisual platforms automatically download the next chapter and social networks use algorithms that obstruct links, with the aim of ensuring you don't leave them, bookshops are now translating that logic to their architecture by filling their floors with temptations, stimuli, and simulacra. Bookshops' biggest adversaries include Facebook, Instagram, Twitter, YouTube, Netflix, LINE, WeChat, or Kakao. The bookshops I've mentioned are fighting back with strategies of their own in the hope of capturing and keeping readers' attention, in an unequal but exciting contest that defines the core of our era.

Against Bibliophilia

Long before it became a book, the Bible was a collection of stories whose heroes were men and women of this world. While the great mythologies of earlier cultures narrated the sphere of the divine and its intersection with the human, the pages of Hebrew mythology reveal layers of dust and rock-like solidity and are inhabited by flesh and blood human beings, with Yahweh as a motionless engine and secondary character, who comes and goes—invisible god or *deus ex machina*—depending on the dramatic structure of each of the books that artificially make up The Book.

Or each author, because long before they were chapters of a single, immense work, Genesis, The Song of Songs, or The Gospel according to St Paul were poems, stories or novels or treatises, legends or biographies, each with its own mother or father. The Bible's unity is a collective illusion, consolidated over centuries by Jewish and Christian readers. Packed into a single volume, it has lost its original form, one much more suited to its content: a shelf of scrolls, with no order or harmony, a cobweb without a centre, and an archive.

The first great publisher in history, consequently, wasn't the brilliant humanist Aldo Manuzio, who created in his Venetian printshop a centre for study, composition, and distribution at the end of the fifteenth and beginning of the sixteenth centuries, but the publisher, or anonymous publishers, academics refer to as "P." As Karen Armstrong explains in *The Bible: A Biography*: "P revised the JE narratives and added the books of Numbers and Leviticus, drawing upon older documents—genealogies, laws and ritual texts—some written down and others orally transmitted." The revolution created by P, who was probably several editors and not a single individual, was spectacular. After they had reread and debated all the more or less sacred materials, it was decided that the verb *shakan* meant "to lead the life of a nomadic tent-dweller," and that, as a result, God didn't want a temple but the desert where his believers lived. Armstrong continues: "In P's revised history, exile was the latest in a sequence of migrations: Adam and Eve had been expelled from Eden; Cain was condemned to a life of homeless vagrancy after murdering Abel; the human race had been scattered at the Tower of Babel; Abraham had left Ur; the tribes had emigrated to Egypt and eventually lived as nomads in the desert." P broadened out the boundaries of the temple *ad infinitum*: from then on, the whole world was a church. Or rather, a book.

P is a step on a long ladder that begins with the first editorial decisions taken by JE. It continues with the additions and reinterpretations made by Ezra and the Jewish translators who translated their sacred texts into Greek during the third century BC, on the island of Pharos, opposite Alexandria. The sects' inventive Jewish-Christian narrators believed in the power of Jesus and decided "to write a completely new collection of sacred texts." This was followed by Origen's allegorical reading, St Jerome's translation (the Vulgate), and the radical changes in selection and editing criteria invoked by Martin Luther and the Protestant revolutionaries.

From the Gutenberg Bible to today, the most famous, most sold, and most influential book—for good and for evil—in the history of humanity has always been adapted to new technologies in the transmission of knowledge. Invented in Italy by Manuzio, the paperback was popularized in seventeenth-century northern Europe by the Elzevir family. Modernity is no longer comprehensible without the format that gave everyone access to knowledge that, for centuries, had been monopolized by clergy and the wealthy. The great metaphor for that democratization is precisely "Bible paper." A very thin, very resistant paper that absorbs ink well and became popular because it was the perfect material for the printing of bibles and dictionaries.

My copy of Armstrong's book has an absurd number of underlinings because I find the history of the Bible so fascinating: the Bible's journey from those handwritten scrolls to the copies in every library (and, in the United States, in the bedside-table drawers of every hotel room). Its strange evolution: in the beginning it was a series of texts that aimed to describe and historicize, let's say: non-fiction; then it transmuted into a sacred anthology—let's say, fiction disguised as non fiction; and was finally accepted as symbolic fiction, let's say, non-fiction disguised as fiction. But beyond theologians' interpretations, it can be read as poetry, epic, novel, or self-help book, because all classics adapt to their readers' eyes at every moment of the future.

I can't imagine having books in my library that I can't underline. Turn the corner of the page. Lend. Pile up. Take to class. Read in the metro or café. Even: lose. That's what I think bibliophilia is: a critical, shared love of books, their history and their stories, of their language and capacity for moral, psychological, spiritual, and intellectual penetration. And that's why I can't understand that other kind of bibliophilia, the collecting of unique, fragile, expensive copies. Books you must read wearing gloves; that you can't lend to a friend; that you must hide like the treasure they are (while telling yourself, with a greedy smirk: "*My* treasure...").

One of the ways to detect an aristocrat in the French Revolution was to examine his library. Leather bindings, often signed by a renowned craftsman, were as expensive as ebony bookshelves. Condorcet might have saved his skin if he'd gotten rid of his valuable copy of Horace, which bore the royal print-shop's seals and thus betrayed him as a fake republican. The first thing the revolutionaries did with the libraries they requisitioned was to remove the books from their showy, heavy, grandiose bindings, which were anathema to the lightness and ease of use that encourage reading.

Since then, millions of us readers have been able to possess our own personal libraries. A library that, like the bookshops it reflects like a complementary mirror, is stylistically and formally diverse, with different front and back covers, flaps, sizes, and a variety of colours, as if the idea of the modern library were still in flight from those noble libraries where every copy was bound according to the taste of a single owner, not the multifarious tastes of their authors and publishers. A democratic library, ruled by a love of reading, a wish to escape or a desire for knowledge, beyond the masquerade of wrappings that may be a sign of artisanal craft, art, and cultural tradition, but are also a distraction from what really matters: content.

Like coin- or stamp-collecting, bibliophilia as a hobby belongs to museums rather than to life. It is an anachronism that takes us back to an era when reading was the exclusive right of an elite. Democracy is, however, that ordering of reality where republics can coexist with monarchies, videogames with horseback riding, space engineers with lumberjacks, YouTubers with cobblers. And the fact is, that if you love books but don't spend a fortune on unique copies or exotic volumes, you'll keep buying other books, paperbacks, new titles, second-hand books, because their pull is tyrannical. If you love books, you'll line your walls with shelves until they're completely covered. If you love books, you'll even soon forget your house had walls. If you love books, in the end you are condemned to be an anachronism, because their price per square metre doesn't allow for infinite libraries. But perhaps we human beings prefer to live in a state of contradiction?

Where Does Paper End and Screen Begin?

∾ A JOURNEY TO SEOUL BESET BY QUESTIONS

> Why?
> Why?
> Why?
>
> Fill a brilliant day with questions
> for five-year-old children
> They surely know
> that without those whys
> everything would be nothing.
>
> —KO UN

I am in South Korea, the land of LG Electronics and Samsung, the land of the Qualcomm Mirasol, Kyobo's e-reader, which allows you to read books in colour. I'm in the country with the highest percentage of citizens with smart cell phones in the world: over 90 percent of South Koreans are connected to social media. I am in a country that has been divided between capitalists and communists since 1948—satellites, respectively, of the US and Soviet Union—and I, too, am divided between wakefulness and sleep. Or rather I'm completely dazed, somewhere between melatonin and jetlag.

I think about all this—not very lucidly—from atop Deoksugung Lottecastle, a block of flats with its own shopping centre and ground-floor bookshop, on my first early morning in Seoul, as I look out the window at a metallic dawn. Darkness around the skyscraper recedes over the terraces in a girls' school sports stadium, as semicircular and venerable as a Roman amphitheatre, opposite the Russian embassy, a massive block packed with parabolic aerials, both spaces surrounded by screens that are lit up night and day.

In Spain, where only 80 percent of the population is connected, it's still yesterday, I decide before falling back to sleep: I have journeyed into the future.

What is that frontier of time actually like? An hourly gradation? Where does the present end and the future begin?

The day he received a call from promoters of Common Ground, a shopping centre made from the world's largest shipping containers, Lee Kiseob was in the new office of his shop, Thanks Books; he'd been forced to leave a larger space, with cafeteria service, due to financial problems.

"I wasn't interested in opening the Common Ground branch of Thanks Books with the same aesthetic and concept, because each area has an identity of its own, and each bookshop must find a way to enter into dialogue with that identity," says this bookseller with round glasses and thick black hair, who keeps smiling in restrained but nervous fashion, "and here we had to develop a concept linked to the university area where we found ourselves and all this metal from containers."

That's why the sliding door is old and wooden: *hanok*, or

traditional Korean house-style. That's why you must climb a few steps and the entire floor is covered in parquet: to mark a transition. Once inside, you encounter metal again, in the tables and shelves.

Index Books has three levels: the top is the cafeteria, where they don't serve espresso, just Index-brand filtered coffee; the middle is the bookshop, which is curated like an art gallery, its books ordered alphabetically with labels like "D for Design," "U for Used," or "W for With"; while the lower floor is devoted to posters, which are arranged in big drawers.

"My *Graphic Magazine* partners and I thought it was the kind of text that, in aesthetic terms, was closest to the containers," says my guide, who is also a graphic designer. "Our posters are single-page books, written by artists, musicians, writers, and designers, and are the main marks of our identity."

Where does a bookseller's identity end and his bookshop's begin? In which arena of negotiation with a building, a district, or a city does the spirit of the bookshop contract or expand?

"In recent years there has been an explosion of independent presses, print magazines, and small bookshops. Opening a small, one-person business linked to books is a good way to escape the neo-liberal pressures of the Korean professional world," says bookseller Cha Kyoung-hee, whose business cards introduce her as "Bookshop Editor."

Although she normally opens at midday, she has offered us her space at 10 a.m. so I can interview Han Kang there. "It's a very literary bookshop, where we'll have quiet," the Korean writer had emailed me the previous night.

Even lifelong Seoul residents can't escape the chaos of the city's postal addresses. "Jorge?" someone had asked a few minutes earlier behind my back. Even Han Kang got lost in the alleyways surrounding this fortress-like building, constructed in the 1950s by North Korean immigrants, despite being a regular customer who'll be back next Tuesday for a reading to mark the publication of her collected stories. We finally reached Goyo Bookshop, sat down with coffee offered by Cha Kyoung-hee, and began our conversation.

She's wearing black jeans, a woollen jersey that's black at the bottom and with the embroidered grey outline of a city skyline at the top. Her hair is dark and lank and she's not wearing makeup: the only touch of colour is the red hands of her watch. She emanates a tense calm that seems to be on the verge of expiring. Everything about her is restrained except for the words that accompany the gentle movements of her hands, which hide a subtle determination. She will be forty-eight next week. She's used to being interviewed.

The author of *The Vegetarian* was vegetarian for a few years, "but I was ill, and my doctor told me to eat fish, though I still don't eat red meat." Although she likes plants, she only has a few because she lives in an apartment and doesn't have a garden. She thinks of herself as a feminist because "you are one if only because you oppose sexism." She likes travel, but not hotels. "They are very lonely places. I prefer staying a long time when I travel, in friends' houses or apartments, in places I find interesting." Seoul is a monster of a city. "It's too big, but I wouldn't exchange it for anywhere quieter, I want to live here, because Korea is the country of my literature."

How can you narrate a country that, in 1948, split permanently into two radically different parts; a country whose landscape is brutally broken? Via novels, films, exhibitions, or chronicles that are also riven and fissured?

Index was established in November 2017. In the final days of 2018, with the temperature slowly but surely descending, I visit other new bookshops. Historybooks, which has a large, iconic history wheel in its window, opened before the summer. And IANN publishers, which has published artbooks since 2007, decided to open a new bookselling space in March: The Reference.

I leaf through *A Blow Up*, by Seung Woo Back, a book of photographs made from fragments of the negatives North Korean censors handed to Back at the border, after cutting out unauthorized images. It took the South Korean photographer years to realize that that mutilated material made for a much more eloquent account of his two-headed country than could have been constructed from the perfect original negatives.

In Seoul Selection, a small space dedicated to books about Korea, located in a basement opposite the Gyeongbokgung Palace and close to Seoul's Museum of Modern and Contemporary Art, I consult the catalogue for the last Gwangu Art Biennale, where recent North Korean art was exhibited for the first time. Many of the works were collective; all were academic: one career option for young people in the world's most hermetic country is that of artist or writer. But in Choe Chang Ho's painting, *In the International Exhibition*, I find an unexpected image: four women, in a nineteenth-century artist's studio, looking at the screen of a Mac laptop. At the centre of socialist realism, the principal emblem of digital capitalism. On the stage of the past, the design of the future.

There was a rapid unfreezing after the Olympic Games were held in PyeongChang: bookshops reflect this changing political temperature. I'm not surprised to see various tourist-themed books and postcards in Veranda Books, the most hipsterish shop I found, a delightful space with an attic ceiling that mostly sells illustrated books, in the neighbourhood with the oldest *hanoks*, and consequently with the most tourists. Now that its citizens have travelled the world, Korea is preparing to become a tourist destination, too. The northern border is one of its main attractions. And the bookshops and libraries, which are springing up everywhere, will soon be attractions as well.

Which surface can most exactly reflect a culture? Which surfaces can or cannot reflect it? Isn't every journey a quest for appropriate spectacles, vantage points, and mirrors?

"Seoul bookshops have changed radically over the last ten years. They all used to be the same, now each has its own distinct identity and is worth a visit," Lee Kiesob tells me before we say goodbye, as three girls take photos in front of a display of Index postcards. One says: "There is always another kind of game."

Several of us cultural tourists are taking selfies in the amazing Starfield Library. Crisscrossed by escalators, this library—opened May 31, 2007—of fifty thousand volumes ranged on as many as twenty-five levels of shelves, with its imperial bookcases and reading tables, occupies the hall and some side areas of the COEX shopping centre. But most visitors are here to meet up or read, not to upload images to Instagram.

We tourists also take photos in the Kyobo bookshop, the most famous in Seoul, admired for the harmonious order of its books—several hundred square metres of them—for its sections selling the latest technology and gifts, and for its cafeterias.

Book Park, located in the Itaewon district's vast Hannam-dong cultural complex (owned by Interpark, the "Korean Amazon"), could become a third tourist icon: there's a sign shaped like a camera indicating the best place to take a photo of its kilometres of vertical bookshelves. A twentieth-century camera, because icons always lag behind reality.

You'll find the same sign in Seoul's Metropolitan Library, next to City Hall, pointing to the spectacular timbered readers' circle that extends down to the library's children's section. A few metres away, in the entrance to Kyobo, now that the good weather has arrived, there are steps filled with people reading books. Book by Book and the Starfield Library also have large wooden steps where you can sit and read.

Conversely, in the huge network of connections that is the Seoul metro, you never see anyone reading a book: cell phones dominate that space, a world frozen in silence.

Where does the city end and theatre begin?

Han Kang puts three volumes of her short stories on the table. "They represent twenty years of stories, and, as you can imagine, they are very important to me." She speaks in English, slowly, but fluently and precisely. These texts connect the adult woman with the young woman who aspired to be a writer. She comes from a poor family, from a house with hardly any furniture, but lots of books: "My father was a young novelist in the '70s and is now a prolific author, but at that time we didn't even have a table to eat off, although we did have a big library, where I enjoyed total freedom to read whatever I wanted: reading was my territory."

When she was in high school, she liked to imagine that Seoul was pronounced like "soul": "I remember buying my first book at the age of seventeen, the start of my own library, in a small bookshop in Suyu-ri, here in Seoul, where I grew up after we moved from Gwangju." It was a book of poems by Han Yong: *Your Silence.*

She began writing poetry as an adolescent; stories in university. In the '90s in Korea you had to win a prize to be considered a proper writer: "I won one organized by an important newspaper, and published some poems in a magazine, and I thus became a writer. The set up isn't so rigid now, but it worked like that then, which might sound odd to someone from Europe." At twenty-eight, she published her first novel—its title could be translated as *Black Horns*—about a woman who disappears. Her fiancé and a girlfriend search for her. I ask Han if she's still happy with it. "It's quite long, four times the length of *The Vegetarian.* I worked on it for three years, it was a profound experience for me, and yes, I do still like it."

Can one person be the best way to approach the soul of a city, of an entire country? Or a bookshop? Or a library? Or an electronic device? Or a book?

Tongmungwan is invisible in the middle of Gwanhun-dong, a bustling street with shops selling handicrafts and souvenirs. A plaque on the façade ("Seoul Future Heritage") and a framed certificate inside attest to its cultural value. Having opened its doors in 1934, it is the oldest bookshop in Korea. Most of the books display Chinese characters, which means that the usual customers aren't so much ordinary Korean readers as academics and collectors from the whole of Asia, particularly from China and Japan. Newspapers, political pamphlets, and other historical documents are also for sale. A representative of the store's third generation of booksellers is behind the counter, at the end of a central passageway formed by metal shelving, literally buried by the books piled up on large, dark, wooden bookcases. Hunched yet proud, Lee Jong-un tells me they only moved once, in 1957, from a few metres down the same street.

At the age of seventeen, Lee Gyeom-no, the bookshop's founder, left his home in what is now North Korea, intending to study in Japan, but an earthquake on the powerful nearby islands put an end to his plans. He stayed in Seoul and started working in an antiquarian bookshop, not out of a love for books—as has so often been repeated—but because he was hungry. Hunger for food can be assuaged, but a hunger for books is insatiable, for good or ill. Over decades, he not only bought and sold books, he published scholars from around the entire country and salvaged stolen documents and books to return or give to the main national libraries. When the bombing raids started, in 1950, Lee had to choose between saving his collection of eighty old books, or his crockery, mattress, or paintings. He didn't hesitate for a second. He died at ninety-seven, four years after paying off a long-overdue debt. In a 2000 meeting of members from the family's two branches, separated for almost half a century by the new border, Lee Gyeom-no met Ryu Ryeol, a bibliophile like himself, but also a sage, and paid Ryu the half million in royalties he owed him for a book he published before the war. After paying his debts, Lee was able to rest in peace.

Could North Korea and South Korea really be the same country in two parallel universes?

If Johannes Gutenberg had travelled to Korea along the Silk Road in the fifteenth century—as had Marco Polo at the end of the previous one—he might have discovered that what he thought of as the future was in fact a version of the past. In July 1377, two craftsmen by the names of Seokcan and Daldam used movable metal type to print *Jikji*, the work in which their master, Baegun Hwasang, summed up the teachings of Zen Buddhism. Eighty years before Gutenberg printed his Bible.

Despite periodic invasions by the Chinese and Japanese, Korean culture was unified and powerful until it split, in the middle of the last century, into simultaneous realities that seemed different but were both equally dictatorial. In the North, under the control of Kim Il-sung, the People's Democratic Republic of Korea was a dictatorship of the proletariat that—like all dictatorships—had a single leader; in the South, the Republic of Korea was also the fief of dubious, neo-liberal conservatives, like President Syngman Rhee and General Park Chung-hee.

While the North sank into poverty, the South experienced an unprecedented economic miracle, leaping in a single generation from the Third to the First World. It was a fast, traumatic transition. Perhaps the day when that trauma is most acutely relived is university entrance-examination day, the famous Suneung, which has become a cruel rite of passage for Korean adolescents. Parents, remembering the hunger they experienced in their childhoods, put all their hopes and too much pressure on their children. After months of studying thirteen hours a day, with a narcotic dearth of sleep, boys and girls stake everything on eight hours of tests. One out of ten Koreans confess to having considered committing suicide in their youth. Among OECD countries, South Korea has the third-highest suicide rate for males and the highest rate for females.

South Korea's is an unusual, lively, still-young democracy. Most of its fifty million inhabitants, half of whom live in Seoul and its metropolitan area, are survivors of war, poverty, dictatorships, and huge stress. It will be a long time before we discover whether North Korea's twenty-five million inhabitants have also survived.

Can realism represent our realities?

If I had to make up a canon for the twenty-first-century novel, limited to ten titles, one would be *The Vegetarian*. This hypnotic story of a woman, who, after deciding not to eat meat, gradually renounces her humanity, to the point of identifying with trees, not only tackles one of the biggest issues of our time—empathy for other living beings, in particular in the vegetable kingdom—it does so while showing great sensitivity to contemporary art, making the most fitting narrative choices in order to relate the protagonist's enigmatic drama. The first part is narrated from the perspective of the husband, who doesn't love his wife; the second, by the latter's brother-in-law, who desires her artistically and sexually; and the final section by her sister, who doesn't know what to do with her. The vegetarian thus remains at the centre of the novel like its dark kernel, a fascinating mystery never to be resolved: "she seemed to be a sacred being, a being you couldn't say was human or animal, or perhaps a being that was somewhere between the vegetable, the human and the animal."

A short story provided the novel's seed: "The Fruit of My Woman," from 1997, was the first version of what would later become the first part of *The Vegetarian*. The story—which can be read on the *Granta* website—tells the story of a man who comes back from a business trip to find his wife in the process of becoming a vegetable. He helps and supports her in her farewell to the human species: "It was the result of a vision, the image of a woman changing into a tree suddenly appeared to me, and although it has moments of light, it is a deeply sad tale."

It is like a contemporary version of the story of Daphne and Apollo: "I didn't think of that until later, when *The Vegetarian* was published in other countries, and people began to speak about the influence of Ovid and Kafka on my work. I read both when I was an adolescent, and I suppose they are still inside me. It's curious," she continues, "how different cultures have found different reference points and asked me very different questions: readers and journalists in Italy were interested in Ovid and the lack of communication; in Germany, in Kafka, and in the sense of what is human, and in violence; in the Anglo-Saxon world, on the other hand, the obsession was feminism; in Spain and Argentina, sacrifice and martyrdom."

"So now I must ask you about Borges," I interject.

"I love Borges," she replies, "he is one of my favourite authors, one of my indispensable reads."

Between story and novel, I note, there is a double twist: the husband's love disappears and the story abandons its fantastic vein and turns realist. "I think that genre is very important if we are to understand those issues, those decisions; poetry is very personal, is closely conditioned by language; as is the short story, but less so, and it's more visual, but I think that the novel is the most important genre because it allows me to ask the most elemental questions." When Han was writing *The Vegetarian*, a question came up that wasn't in "The Fruit of My Woman": the meaning of humanity. "Although I've wondered ever since I was a child about what it means to be a human being, because I don't find it at all natural, I find it hard to accept that I belong to the human species, that I belong to the same kind of animal that built Auschwitz or perpetrated the Gwangju Massacre." Her intention was to emphasize that the protagonist's decision, to cease to be human, is understood by no one, but that she won't give up on what she has decided. "And the fact is I don't think I opted for realism, or that *The Vegetarian* is a realist novel exactly."

Is this chronicle only realist in the fragments between the question marks?

In the Book by Book bookshop they give you a cup of American coffee if you write a review of a book you liked on one of the big cards they've set aside, the ancient bartering practice contrasting with that of the banking offices that occupy 50 percent of the space.

Near City Hall, around the bar at the Café Comma, a giant bookcase packed with books reaches to the ceiling and is reflected in the window opposite, where poetry collections with colourful covers are on display. A girl in a school uniform says hello while I leaf through one; for a second I assume she's a student, but her name is on a badge on her chest: she's an assistant in the clothing store where the café-bookshop is located—her colleagues all wear the same uniform.

Back atop of Deoksugung Lottecastle, on my last day in Seoul, I wake to a city I don't recognize. The girls' school amphitheatre, the Russian embassy's parabolic aerials, and the skyscraper screens are about to disappear under a thick layer of white. Although snow in November is unusual, on my way to the airport I note how quickly the municipal machinery has gone into action: concierges from the blocks of flats are clearing pathways and plows are removing ice from the motorways along which we cross the megalopolis before reaching Incheon. After checking in and going through security, I'm not surprised to end up breakfasting in a delightful café-bookshop that shares a space with tax-refund counter: Sky Book Cafe versus Tax Refund, while a white robot with two pink hearts instead of eyes slides between them on wheels with a message on the screen: "I love you."

The crises all bookshops face are similar, but each city confronts its crisis in its own way. Seoul has imposed an unexpected hybridity: a bookshop selling posters in a shopping centre made from shipping containers; a bookshop and a bank branch; a bookshop and a clothing store; a bookshop and an airport. Four responses to the same question, in a city that seems to exist in humanity's next decade.

How can we guarantee the survival of future bookshops?

Andrés Felipe Solano, a Colombian writer who has been exploring Seoul passionately and meticulously for the last ten years, gives me the latest issue of the magazine of Korea's Literary Translation Institute, where he works cheek by jowl with Spanish-to-Korean translators. Its editorial makes it clear that the prestigious International Man Booker Prize won by Han Kang and her translator, Deborah Smith, for *The Vegetarian*, represents a watershed in the history of the country's literature. Here there is no consensus that it is a masterpiece, but it has certainly been recognized as an important work of fiction in its various versions in other languages. The publication also confirms that, for South Korea, English is as key a language as Chinese or Japanese.

That same truth is repeated on the five storeys of Still Books, the capital's most refined, postmodern bookshop, the ground floor of which currently stocks all English issues of *Brand* magazine. On the top floor you can taste the best Japanese whiskies. Walking between themed tables where books coexist with designer items; going backwards or forwards downstairs or across brown parquet floors with tiny displays of maps, pictures, and photographs at intersections, you realize that the bookshop's centre of gravity is the city of Seoul itself; that the Korean language and Korean culture are arrayed around this protagonist, but that Anglo-Saxon, Chinese, and Japanese culture interest booksellers as much as customers. Their readers.

I buy the issue of *Brand* dedicated to Tsutaya, the bookshop chain that defines itself as the main "Japanese platform for pop culture." Like Amazon or Fnac, it was born primarily as a bookstore, but unlike those companies it hasn't relegated books to the background. In its television and computer departments, so I read, you will find thousands of books on technology; and in the kitchenware department, gastronomic books. Each

AGAINST AMAZON

year, dozens of new franchises open, but the structure grows from its bookish base. Even its most iconic architecture, like the T-Site headquarters (designed by Klein Dytham architecture), is inspired by that icon, that symbol, that minimal unit of cultural meaning from recent centuries; and, who knows, perhaps also of future centuries: the book.

Tsutaya's closest equivalent in Korea might be the Kyobo bookshop chain, which was born in the 1980s as a gamble on cultural industries wagered by the insurance company of the same name. "People create books, books create people" is written in huge letters across a wall in one of its branches. Although Kyobo's ten branches offer thousands of books and items, arranged in themed sections, the shop's most emblematic space is its library, where, from 9:30 a.m., huge wooden tables are filled with people reading newspapers and students of all ages leaning over their open books. Tsutaya's T-Site, similarly, features the Anjin Library, which has one hundred and twenty seats and an impressive collection of magazines. Even the walkway that connects the bookshop's three buildings is called Magazine Street.

Still Books sells a guide to Seoul's bookshops in the original Korean and in Japanese translation, as well as three guides to Japanese bookshops with titles in English: *New Standard of Japanese Bookstores*, *Tokyo Bookstore Guide*, and *Tokyo Book Scene*. I look carefully at the photos in the four volumes: it's obvious that Tokyo's bookshops are similar to the ones I've visited in Seoul over the last few days. I jot down the names of some I will surely add to my collection in the future: Isseido, Beyer, Shibuya Publishing & Booksellers, Los Papelotes, Orion Papyrus, Sunday Issue, Book and Bed, Sanyodo Book Store, Kitazawa, Book and

Sons. There are always one or several books in the run-up to a journey. And a list.

Even Bunkitsu, the Tokyo bookshop that opened its doors in 2018 and became the first in history to charge for entry from day one, has an unexpected twin soul in Seoul. Because that exhaustive collection of magazines and art, architecture, and design books—which share space with tables for both group and individual use (no doubt inspired by the New York Public Library or National Library in Buenos Aires, with their renowned green lamps)—doesn't resemble Index as much as the Hyundai Car Design Library. In effect: it's more a library than a bookshop.

Seoul and Tokyo look at each other across the mirror of the Sea of Japan. The burden of the history of violence between the two countries remains, Japan's past abuses still palpitate and bleed, but the bookshops seem to be meeting places, areas of peace—at least in illustrations and photos and on the maps.

Where does a chronicle finish and an essay begin? Where does a chronicle that's an essay or an essay that narrates end, and where does fiction begin?

The image of the metamorphosis of the protagonist in "The Fruit of My Woman" was so powerful that Han Kang wanted to continue working on it, but she wasn't ready for that project and another came her way: her second novel, which could be translated as *Cold Hands*. It was only then that she felt ready to tackle the writing of the third, *The Vegetarian*, a story that would be read throughout the world. It was published in 2007 and the prize was given to the English translation in 2016: "It was strange to have to talk about it again, because I'd already disconnected from that book, though then I ended up re-thinking it a lot as a result of my conversations with translators, publishers, and journalists, who taught me a lot."

Korea's National Museum of Modern and Contemporary Art is currently exhibiting work by Yun Hyong-keun dedicated to the memory of the Gwangju Massacre, in which over a thousand citizens died at the hands of dictator Park Chung-hee's army: canvasses where large, dark patches are fractured by streaks of white. The massacre is central to *Human Acts*, Han Kang's fourth novel, also translated into English by Deborah Smith. "In my opinion, the two novels are very connected, because the theme of violence is central to both, but I am sure *Human Acts* is a more personal novel, the most personal I have written."

I say its complex structure made me think of Claude Lanzmann's *Shoah* and a film that is in some way its heir, Rithy Panh's *S-21: The Khmer Rouge Killing Machine*, as well as the great writers on the memory of genocide, like Paul Celan. "I'm very interested in *The Periodic Table* by Primo Levi, and his other books that show it is possible to write about Auschwitz. I've also read Paul Celan's work, an extraordinary writer, but my essential reading for *Human Acts* was a Korean book of eyewitness accounts by survivors of Gwangju. I read it in one month, in nine-hour daily sessions, and cried over every page, but before experiencing that, I was lost, I didn't know how to tackle the novel, and after a month of reading and weeping, the structure came to me and I was able to start writing."

In its mother tongue, a book has a different rhythm than in translation. While she was launching those novels in various countries, Han enacted performances here related to her latest book, entitled *The White Book*, where, through fragments that draw on poetry, narrative, and essays, she speaks about her sister, who died a few hours before she was born. An eighteen-minute video was made from the four performances she did in 2016, in which other performers also participate: "although they are independent of the book, there is a clear metaphorical relationship, I am trying to understand how mourning works."

Could all these new bookshops and libraries in Seoul be a symptom, a reaction, a form of mourning?

In an era when libraries tend to be huge spaces crisscrossed with multimedia outlets, I am surprised to find four small, specialized laboratories in Seoul's Hyundai Card libraries. In an era when libraries have filled up with people looking for a bookish atmosphere in which to immerse themselves in their screens, these four libraries allow people to consult books in relation to objects that give them meaning: the texts lead to physical acts rather than to technology. In the Design, Cookery, Music, and Travel libraries, books continue to be the protagonists.

The Design Library is like a small contemporary art museum, with a central garden that articulates the building's three floors. Its three areas are arranged according to the classical criteria of library science: the first has contemporary art books, museum catalogues, periodical publications, and volumes on industrial design; these are also present in the third area, together with architecture, public and organic interior design and photography books; while in the second we find bibliographies on book design, marketing, visual communication, user design, and assorted other titles. For example, in a tiny corner on the second floor, next to a small room with views over the roofs of neighbourhood *hanoks*, is a selection of some twenty books on smallness: sinks, miniatures, minimalism, and micro-apartments.

In order for a book to be selected for the Design Library, it must be inspiring, useful, communicative, influential, a bridge between different media, an actual or potential classic, and beautiful. The rest of these libraries have also made public the guidelines their respective curators follow when selecting their catalogue titles. What makes the project unique isn't any sort of new concept of the library as a repository for books, but rather the curating and *mise en scène* that generate a completely different atmosphere to what we'd find in a design faculty library. Architecture and small details have been used to create an experience that is at once different, sensuous, artisanal, and pleasant. Next to reading tables and armchairs you find a coffee-maker and a fridge full of bottled water. On every surface where you might place your book you find wooden boxes of Faber Castell pencils and blank sheets of paper. Everything has been conceived and chosen so the reader feels like a privileged being who will enjoy the possibility of translating his or her reading into notes, drawings, or future projects.

Each of the four libraries offers different bookmarks, with an undeniable value placed on the tactile and designer qualities of the paper used. The pamphlet explaining the Hyundai Card libraries is exquisite, the print book being at the centre of each experience: art, crafts, and design bibliographies in the Design Library; recipe books, books on raw materials or gastronomy in the Cookery Library: travel literature, maps, guide books, or *National Geographic*'s entire run in the Travel Library: biographies of singers, musicological essays, scores, and musical titles in the Music Library.

Interfaces that allow reading to be transformed into experience and memory are located nearby. Those Design Library pencils. Those records and gramophones in the Music Library (on sale in the next-door shop, Vinyl & Plastic). Those interactive maps in the Travel Library. Those trays and pans, stoves and cookers in the Cooking Library. The reader becomes a maker. In that stimulating context, knowledge doesn't derive from YouTube or Wikipedia, but from a book, generally chosen with a partner or friends. Thanks to the map, gramophone, café or restaurant table, reading becomes collective, a group experience, an experiment with the five senses.

The four libraries have inner structures that suggest mobile homes. In Design, the suggestion is of a wood cabin; in Travel, it's a ceiling in the form of a crooked hive, recalling a bed-and-breakfast attic room; in Music there are modules that evoke the privacy of a bedroom where adolescents can create their own soundtrack (and a concert hall or discotheque), and in Cooking there's a kind of outdoor greenhouse that acts as both a dining room and interior greenhouse, which classifies and displays all manner of ingredients.

It's about offering secure, silent spaces where skills and knowledge can be developed that are not one's own, the company's or the academy's. That are practical but linked to domestic life, to leisure, to reading for pleasure in the warmth of a semi-public, shared hearth, and not to a professional career or the direct conversion of work into money. Although access is via credit card.

Where does paper end and screen begin?

Before saying goodbye, I ask Han Kang for her favourite book-shops: "I love visiting small bookshops, like this one, Goyo; like Thanks Books, like wit n cynical, which specializes in poetry, or The Book Society."

And that's where I go. The Book Society was launched in the Sangsu-dong district in 2010 by Helen Ku and Lim Kyung Yong, who had run a small art-book imprint, mediabus, for two years. Located on the first floor above a Jongno-gu garage, the shop has an art gallery atmosphere. "Right from the start," Lim tells me, "we have focused on events that create a sense of community, concerts, artistic events, launches, and conversations."

It was here, the Spanish writer Lourdes Iglesias tells me, that she and her husband, Bartomeu Marí, who directed Korea's National Museum of Modern and Contemporary Art for three years, first made contact with the local scene. "We want to find bridges," continues Lim Kyung Yong, "between the world of print, artifacts, and human and digital networks, and that's why we are translating and making available the most important works of critical theory in English in Korean."

Irasun Books, in a nearby passageway, can be defined with two key words: Photobook and Booktalk. The shop's warm interior displays photography books from the world's best publishers; half a dozen people are reading or conversing quietly.

These small bookshops aren't easy to find. Like many in Seoul, they're in alleyways, side-streets, or nowhere at all, because they can't afford the rents paid by the ever-present cosmetics or electronic-goods shops.

You reach Alibaba, a second-hand bookshop with a post-apocalyptic-bunker aesthetic similar to Kyobo's in Gangnam, from a lift that descends to the basement of a commercial building. Opposite the lift are large tables where readers consult books or take notes. Genuine Gangnam style is underground.

Where does a reply end and the next question begin? Which border unites and separates on each journey? Isn't every text a layering of strata, a succession of questions and answers?

The publisher Seung-hwan Lee—whose professional patter emanates from the face of an adolescent—tells me paper sales account for about 80 percent of the Korean market, digital 20 percent, but that some books are print-only "because the Korean reader likes to touch and feel"; which is why sophisticated cover and interior book design was the common denominator in all the bookshops I visited.

In this polluted city, where many people wear masks as they move around, the paths and parks that are continually being built are absolutely vital. For the same reason, in this digital city, where so many buildings have huge screens and ten million cell phones are in perpetual movement, it makes total sense that bookshops and reading spaces are multiplying. But those readers are a minority: South Korea isn't just the country with the most web surfers in the world, it's also the country with the lowest number of readers on the planet. While Indians read an average of ten hours a week, and the Spanish almost six, Koreans don't get beyond three.

All the innovative libraries and hybrid bookshops that have opened in Seoul in recent years might just be a fashion or fad with a best-before date. Or possibly they're an attempt to make South Korea more appealing for tourists. But they can also be interpreted as an attempt to put things right.

In twenty years, an economic miracle changed a poor country into a very rich country; an economy without an entrepreneurial base became a leading economy in electronic goods, cosmetics, and automobiles. Antiquated schools and universities transformed into an educational system that is as successful as it is dangerously competitive. The future arrived so quickly it didn't take account of the absence of a past. Around the world, public and private book collections comprised a physical and mental, critical and democratic structure, which was then gradually digitized. Here it's happening in reverse. I didn't really travel to the future, but to the past that should have preceded it, and that South Korea is now forging. Or inventing.

> North South East West: making no distinction
> covering everywhere alike,
> in white, no one can keep back
> the snowstorm.
>
> —KIM KWANG-KYU
>
> *(Translated by Brother Anthony of Taizé and Kim Young-moo)*

The Future of Libraries

I   BOOK BURNING

Ray Bradbury, who graduated from high school but didn't go to university, honed his narrative talents in the theatres and studios of Hollywood, and sharpened his intellect amid the bookshelves of the Los Angeles Public Library. As his family couldn't afford to send him to university, Bradbury began visiting different sections of the public library as an adolescent and avidly read everything put before him until he was twenty-seven. The library, he wrote later, was "my birthing place; it was my growing place."

It's hardly surprising then that he wrote his novel *The Fireman*, which would ultimately be called *Fahrenheit 451*, in another library: UCLA's Powell Library. He suffused the book's characters, scenes, and words with a disturbing notion: in the future, books will be banned, firemen will spend their time burning down libraries, and readers who want to defend culture will have no choice but to memorize texts before they are turned to ash.

A descendent of Mary Bradbury, who was tried for witchcraft in the seventeenth century as one of the notorious witches of

Salem, Ray Bradbury never imagined that, thirty years after his most famous novel was published, the library where he grew as a reader and writer would suffer a devastating fire. Or that, forty years later, the great American journalist Susan Orlean would write about it in the pages of *The Library Book*, a long narrative essay on the Los Angeles Public Library before, during, and after the fire. Or even less that Orlean, author of *The Orchid Thief*, while researching the book, would conclude that she had to experience a book burning first-hand and so decided to destroy, for this purpose, a copy of *Fahrenheit 451*.

II   SOCIAL VOCATION

The Library Book has a fake hero (Harry Peak, the dreamer who may have lit the match in 1986) and dozens of genuine heroes, writers like Ray Bradbury, arson experts, the author's family (including Orlean's mother), and, above all, librarians. Like all good books, structure mirrors subject here as a net intertwining the lives, knowledge, and minor adventures of present-day librarians with those who preceded them in the task of giving spiritual, cultural, and social support to the citizens of Los Angeles.

Orlean has constructed a detective story based on the main arson suspect, and yet that narrative line is the least important aspect of the book, which is impressive primarily as a cultural history of the library—from its dusty origins in a desert city to the day before yesterday—and for its scrutiny of the complex nature of an institution of this kind: a machine within which every department and staff member in the central library and its seventy-two branches collaborates in order to bring books and culture to four million inhabitants.

Current director John Szabo is very clear that the library isn't simply a collection of books, but "a sleek ship of information and imagination"; one that in the near future must become "a fusion of a people's university, a community hub and an information base, happily partnered with the internet rather than in competition with it." Reading Szabo's opinions, and those of so many other individuals in the book, it's obvious that a global conversation is now taking place about the meaning of books and the spaces they occupy. It's a conversation with recurring questions: what cultural objects should a library collect and lend? How can reading be encouraged? How does the library relate to the internet? Should it extend its cultural vocation to providing social support? Echoes from possible responses resound in every city, on every continent.

Szabo says that, apart from the obvious consulting and lending of books and other cultural objects, the institution he directs must also offer cultural and literacy programmes, voting registration, storytimes, computer access, and homelessness outreach. Although one only has to visit the Jaume Fuster Library in Barcelona to understand how libraries have become essential spaces in the lives of a city's homeless, it was last year, in the new Library at the Dock on Melbourne's seafront, when I saw how a building's design can reconcile its traditional mission (cataloguing, cultural advising, studying, and lending) with the social mission it has always fulfilled, but now embraces with complete conviction. Alongside multi-use rooms, many equipped with the tools and materials necessary for different handicrafts, the Australian library now has information counters for immigrants and refugees, English-language classrooms, a large reception area, and a café.

For millions of people throughout the world with few or no resources, libraries have become one of the few hospitable spaces in the cities where they live or are passing through. Orlean calls this "the commitment to inclusion." In increasingly conservative cities, libraries can become embassies, or reminders of solidarity and progress. Because, as the author of *The Library Book* also says, what is happening in libraries is truly miraculous. They are spaces occupied "peacefully, with total understanding, by a mass of strangers." Strangers from different social classes, with books and internet at home, or without those things and homeless, who cohabit with books, DVDs, comics, computers, games, daily newspapers, and magazines. Democracy is particularly visible in libraries. That is why they must be defended.

III   THE FUTURE IS IN THE PAST

Although Susan Orlean's docufiction is entirely regional, focusing on a Californian city and its position in the United States, in its final pages she broadens her range and travels to northern Europe to attend the 2015 biennial Next Library Congress, held in the Dokk1 library in Aarhus, Denmark. This was at once an intellectual and political gesture. On the one hand, Orlean wants to see the object of her study, the Los Angeles Public Library, as part of a network of similar projects; on the other, viewing American cultural institutions from the shores of Europe or through the Bill and Melinda Gates Foundation's Global Libraries Initiative (which financed library activities in fifty countries up to the end of 2018), allows her to defend the importance of public libraries in the context of corporate universities and an education and culture that is being increasingly privatized.

While Orlean attends talks on the latest tendencies in librarianship and archiving, the reader is reminded of dozens of individuals and initiatives from the last one hundred and fifty years that have been described in the book and seem just as, or even more, modern as those under discussion in the Next Library Congress. Anecdotes, biographies, and facts demonstrate how libraries have always been laboratories for innovation.

For example, the Los Angeles Public Library's third director, Mary Foy, a pioneer of the feminization of librarianship that took place in the last quarter of the nineteenth century (it wasn't a coincidence that, after being sacked in 1884, after four years in the post, she became a schoolteacher and suffragette), included among her functions locating documents and chasing lenders who returned their books late (she appears in photos with the leather purse where she kept the fines), as well as "refereeing their chess and checker games, which were played all day long in the reading room." Another of the book's secondary characters, Tessa Kelso, suggested, in the 1880s, that "the Los Angeles Public Library should lend tennis rackets and indoor games." And in the 1920s, "the children's story hour, which was known as Joy Hours for the Wee Folks" attracted a large audience of mothers, children, and nannies. It wasn't just at the most recent turn of the century that libraries became places for games and families: they've been expanding from books to all those spaces that shape us as human beings for a very long time.

"A craze for self-improvement and reinvention thrived in this fresh new place conjured out of the desert," Orlean notes. Various generations of immigrants found in that library the tools to perform ethical or professional surgery on themselves. Aspiring Hollywood actors found film-star memoirs or acting-technique handbooks there; Italians or Latin Americans, books to perfect their English; future secretaries, volumes to teach them typing or bookkeeping; all newcomers, telephone directories and maps to locate their hopes and design strategies for social progress. Long before tutorials appeared on YouTube, libraries were *the* place to go for autodidacts.

That meshing of libraries and society didn't only translate into diverse leisure or educational activities. In the middle of the last century, the American Library Association created "workshops against the Bolshevik threat in order to safeguard users from anti-patriotic thoughts," which it styled as "How to fight Red deception." Today we'd call that "fake news." And the Teen Department was born in 1968, at a time when global awareness was growing about the widening generation gap. The library not only started to stock books for young people, but also organized activities like judo classes or folk and rock concerts (and, a few years later, programming on sexuality, suicide, drug abuse, gangs, and runaways).

"Libraries are society's original co-working spaces and have the distinct advantage of being free," we read in *The Library Book*. In fact, they have been a space for sharing tasks and knowledge from the very first library in Alexandria, which was at once a translation workshop, academy, sanctuary, museum, and archive. In the heart of that institution's origins, we find the mix of everything that shapes the human brain. From the moment it was burnt down, we have been recreating and reinventing those spaces that define, like no other, the best of humanity. Expanses of light that for over two thousand years have tried to compensate for our surfeit of shadows.

COVID-19 *and Bookshops*

Sant Jordi, Catalonia's day of books and roses, the day when Cervantes and Shakespeare died 404 years ago, World Book Day—this April 23, 2020, will be one of the strangest in our lifetime. Because the books and flowers given as gifts, the bookshops spilling out onto street stalls, and the fiestas energizing bodies and cities belong to the shared world of the senses, the world of hugs and crowds. And April 23, 2020, will take place on webpages and social media, cell phones and computer screens. Some of us will be fortunate enough to kiss and exchange books inside the same house. But many will be physically isolated. Anyone intending to use a messenger service to obtain their book or rose should ask themselves, before clicking: do I really want to remember that this came to me via a man wearing gloves and a mask, a man compelled to endanger his life in exchange for a pittance?

My response was that I didn't, which is why I have already bought my books directly from my favourite bookshops. I'll collect them as soon as confinement ends. I imagine I will always remember that moment: re-encountering my booksellers, as I will always remember the first time we returned to the park or beach. Both libelista.com and todostuslibros.com are two good tools for making those purchases, investing today so that the bookshops will be there tomorrow.

Now that this force majeure has closed bookshops, all the players in the book industry have reminded us of their importance. The best support initiatives for booksellers have come from publishers like Comanegra or Nórdica, on whose webpages you can buy books and indicate which bookshop you want to receive the 30 or 35 percent of their cost. The Barcelona publishing house calls the program "Adopt a bookshop"; Nórdica's Madrid bookshop adds, "Bookshops, we miss you. And we want you to return. Every single one."

Less successful are the #LlibreriesObertes projects, from the Mortensen design studio and Som publishing group, and #YoApoyoALasLibrerías ("I Support Bookshops"), from the Penguin Random House group. Both campaigns are palpably suspect. While the llibreriesobertes.cat page has helped many small Catalan bookshops sell books in advance and gain small amounts of liquidity, the Mortenson and Som initiative retains half of their income until the shops reopen and holds onto all data from the transactions. Under the guise of *storytelling* (the central theme being altruism) the companies have obtained a substantial injection of capital and Big Data from thousands of Catalan readers.

And the giant PRH group, while organizing a generous special distribution service so bookshops can sell titles from lists like Lumen, Reservoir Books, and Grijalbo, has at the same time boosted the direct sale of books through its webpage. The contradiction is obvious. When you find a book that interests you at megustaleer.com, you're given six purchasing options: via that website, todostuslibros.com, amazon.es, casadellibro.com, Fnac, and El Corte Inglés. Perhaps that's because all those conglomerate options are equally valid in the eyes of the corporation; although it is currently distributing coupons for a 10 percent discount in bookshops once they reopen, it has removed the hashtag #YoApoyoALasLibrerías from Twitter. It has, however, retained #YoMeQuedoEnCasaLeyendo ("I Stay at Home Reading"), which is undoubtedly closer to the truth.

Llibreries Obertes could have directly supported Catalan bookshops that have webpages set up for electronic sales. PRH could have done the same with pages like todostuslibros.com, which assemble the information necessary to buy directly from thousands of Spanish bookshops. At the moment of truth—the moment of this pandemic—neither large enterprises nor the people responsible for cultural policy are reacting adequately to the situation. Nor, I fear, are bookshops, which aren't organizing or uniting at a time when their existence is truly threatened. Some dispatch books to private homes and others don't; some are still communicating with their community through Instagram, or have digitized their educational courses on Zoom, like the Rafael Alberti in Madrid or Nollegiu in Barcelona, though many haven't. A few, like 80 Mundos in Alicante, have ventured into crowdfunding; others, like Caótica in Sevilla, have advertised for financial partners in order to survive, but most haven't done those things.

Although the pandemic hit Spain two weeks before it reached the US, the few Spanish bookshops organizing fundraising campaigns or issuing calls for help did so after City Lights had already started to do just that. The legendary Beat bookshop, founded in 1953 by Lawrence Ferlinghetti (who turned 101 on March 24) quickly amassed half a million dollars. At the end of last year, Lam Wing Kee, the Hong Kong bookseller, crowd-funded 180,000 euros in order to launch his new bookshop in Taiwan. Lam was one of the five booksellers arrested by the Chinese government in 2015 in Hong Kong for selling and sending out banned books. Thirty police burst into his shop, Causeway Bay Books. On April 25, he will launch the new base for his project in Taipei. There will be no party; the Taiwanese government advises against social gatherings.

Why do people donate money to Caótica, 80 Mundos, City Lights, or Causeway Bay Books? Because they believe in the key nature of their brands and narratives. Design studios, media agencies, and marketing departments use the word "bookshop" in their campaigns because it is an excellent brand. Corporate promotion experts know you must never associate your brand with a less prestigious one, that all alliances must be based on equality or aspiration. The moment you link your brand to the word "bookshop," you harness positive attitudes from many, many people and automatically grab the attention of the mass media and social networks. Bookshops are part of our heritage, but they can also go viral.

Amazon was the first to appropriate the legitimacy, importance, and significance of books and bookshops, exactly a quarter of a century ago. What Jeff Bezos identified in the mid-nineties as a niche market, a sales space that hadn't been picked up by any electronic trading enterprise, was—conversely—the culture and intellectual and emotional fatherland for millions of individuals. Ten years later Google Books arrived on the scene with the same eagerness to appropriate that extraordinarily valuable symbolic cultural capital. Despite the proliferation of books and films about booksellers and bookshops; despite photographs of bookish spaces and reading moments going viral on social media; despite the transformation of several bookshops around the world into tourist icons, bookshops don't seem to have grasped that their brand is extremely powerful, and much more so than those of the giant publishing groups and distributors supplying them, or the political institutions regulating them. Much bigger, even, than Google Books or Amazon. But they have to react. The huge tech companies are earning vast sums of money in these catastrophic times, which they are investing in strategies to render themselves—they hope—even more indispensable. Every day more brains are monopolized by Jeff Bezos, whose aim isn't to be the *prime*, but the *only* option.

Obviously there isn't the same structure of grants for supporting culture in the Hispanic world as exists in Anglo-Saxon culture. The Book Trade Charity has been helping booksellers for 180 years and has just raised over £50,000, to be distributed in the form of scholarships, for those affected by the pandemic. On March 23, 2020, three London publishers created a crowdfunding project to help bookshops. Their aim was to reach £10,000, a figure that rose to £100,000 in just a few days after they received the support of the Booksellers Association and—voilà—of Penguin Random House. But I refuse to accept that structures of solidarity, creativity, or innovation don't also exist within our culture.

The renowned Chinese actor Yao Chen shared with his 83 million followers on the Weibo social network a moving post by the director of the OWSpace bookshop chain, who confessed that they might go bankrupt in six months: "Our hope is that every individual and bookshop will finally emerge from this solitude and embrace the Spring." And the bookshop lover Aakanksha Gaur, owner of the Shelfjoy Instagram account, has created the Save Your Bookstore app, where you can find thousands of bookshops across the world, and purchase their gift tokens with one click.

In these times when millions of us are under house arrest and missing our bookshops, millions of isolated, masked readers who—though communicating via WhatsApp, working on Skype, and devouring stories on Netflix and HBO—have found ideas, escapism, and above all consolation, in our excess of books, bookshops need to react vigorously. They need to re-appropriate the culture of the book. Become conscious of their prestige and power. Ensure their brand and story are valued. What's at stake is their future, which, to a considerable extent, is our future, too.

Acknowledgements

I would like to list the origins of the travel essays and chronicles (sometimes published under other titles) and would like to thank for their support: Eliezer Budasoff, Elías López, Albinson Linares, Pere Ortin, Mario Trigo, Toño Angulo, Iker Seisdedos, Ángel Fernández, Toni Soler, Cristina Vila, Marcelo Cohen, Eugenia de la Torre, Daniel Gascón, Mar de Marchis, and Graciela Speranza, who were their first publishers: "Las mejores librerías del mundo no son las que tú crees" (*The New York Times en Español*, July 15, 2018); "Viaje al final de la luz. Caminando por Londres con Iain Sinclair" (*Altaïr Magazine*, December 2016, Mañé y Flaquer Prize for Travel Journalism 2017); "Las bibliotecas más importantes del mundo" (*The New York Times en Español*, January 27, 2019); "Desarticulo mi biblioteca" (*El Estado Mental*, March 2014); "Las librerías mitológicas de David B." (under the title "Los misterios de París," in *Revista de Libros*, September 2016); "Del Little Havana a Miamizuela" (*The New York Times en Español*, September 16, 2018); "Mi Buenos Aires libresco. Una entrevista a Alberto Manguel en la Biblioteca Nacional de Argentina" (*Jot Down Magazine*, June 2018); "Ese interrogante que llamamos librería" (*El País Semanal*, December 8, 2013); "Bibliotecas de ficción" (*El món d'ahir*, December 2018); "Los perros de Capri" (*The New York Times en Español*, August–September 2017); "En defensa de las librerías" (*El País*, January 3, 2016); "Librerías de viejo versus librerías de nuevo: Una conversación con Luigi Amara,"

Otra parte, 2016); "Contra la bibliofilia" (*Jot Down Magazine*, June 2018); y "¿Dónde acaba el papel y empieza la pantalla? Viaje a Seúl entre signos de interrogación" (*Altaïr Magazine*, March 2019; with a fragment of "Las bibliotecas experimentales de Seúl," CCCB Lab, December 4, 2018), and "Las librerías se reinventan en Tokio" (*The New York Times en Español*, June 30, 2019). "Fuego en la gran biblioteca" (*La Vanguardia*, July 24, 2019).

About the Author

JORGE CARRIÓN'S *Bookshops: A Reader's History*, published by Biblioasis in 2017, was universally acclaimed and has appeared in thirteen languages. He is the author of three novels, including *Los muertos*, which won the 2011 Festival de Chambéry Prize for best first novel in Spanish. Carrión's journalism appears in the Spanish-language edition of the *New York Times* and many other newspapers in Europe and the Americas. He lives in Barcelona, where he is the director of the creative writing program at Pompeu Fabra University.

About the Translator

PETER BUSH'S recent translations include Teresa Solana's *The First Prehistoric Serial Killer and Other Stories*, his selection of *Barcelona Tales*, and Quim Monzó's *Why, Why, Why?* In press are Josep Pla's *Salt Water* and Juan Francisco de Dios Hernández's *Leonardo Balada: A Transatlantic Gaze*; in process, Balzac's *The Lily in the Valley* and Najat El Hachmi's *Mother of Milk and Honey*. He lives in Oxford, UK.